Your Family Heritage

Projects in Appliqué

TERRECE BEESLEY
AND TRICE BOERENS

Martingale & COMPANY

BOTHELL, WASHINGTON

Credits
President . . . . . Nancy J. Martin
CEO/Publisher . . . . . Daniel J. Martin
Associate Publisher . . . . . Jane Hamada
Editorial Director . . . . . Mary V. Green
Technical Editor . . . . . Sharon Rose
Copy Editor . . . . . Candie Frankel
Proofreader . . . . . Leslie Phillips
Cover Designer . . . . . Michael Rohani
Text Designer . . . . . Stan Green
Illustrator . . . . . Terrece Beesley
Cover Photographer . . . . . Brent Kane

Martingale & COMPANY

That Patchwork Place®

MISSION STATEMENT

We are dedicated to providing quality products and service by working together to inspire creativity and to enrich the lives we touch.

Martingale & Company
PO Box 118
Bothell, WA 98041-0118 USA
www.patchwork.com

That Patchwork Place is an imprint of Martingale & Company.
Printed in China
05 04 03 02 01 00 6 5 4 3 2 1

Library of Congress Cataloging-in-Publication Data

Beesley, Terrece.
Your family heritage : projects in appliqué / Terrece Beesley, Trice Boerens.
p. cm.
ISBN 1-56477-308-6
1. Appliqué—Patterns. 2. Quilting—Patterns. I. Boerens, Trice. II. Title.
TT779 .B438 2000
746.46'041—dc21 00-022292

Contents

Introduction

"When love and skill come together, expect a masterpiece."
—Unknown

In the eighteenth and nineteenth centuries, our foremothers spent hours creating needlework samplers. Alphabets and the dates of weddings and births were typical elements in these intricate, beautiful works. Stitching a sampler was a way for a needleworker to pay homage to the events, people, and places that held special meaning for her.

The fast and easy fabric "samplers"* in this book have the same old-fashioned, timeless charm. You'll write in the names and dates important to you to create a custom keepsake for family or friends. Like their antique counterparts, these appliqué samplers are meant to be displayed on the walls of your home.

To get started, choose a design from among the ten beautiful projects in this book. Be sure to pick a design with space for the names you want to include, whether a newlywed couple or three generations of family members. You can also adapt a design to suit your needs. Select fabrics that are similar to those in our photographs, or play around with different combinations for a truly unique piece. Include a piece of cotton from Mom's favorite dress or a scrap from one of Dad's ties to make your sampler more precious to everyone. If you have little ones around, have them write in their own names for a lasting memento of their younger years.

We used fusible interfacing in many of the projects to make them quick and easy—perfect for gift giving when someone's birthday "sneaks up" on you. When you want the immediate satisfaction that comes from finishing a project in one day, you'll find the "Moon and Stars Sampler" a good choice. If you prefer to savor your stitches and see your project evolve slowly, try the "House Sampler" or "Family Tree Sampler."

We hope that *Your Family Heritage* will inspire you to create heirlooms your family will enjoy for years to come.

Terrece Beesley and *Trice Boerens*

*Not to be confused with sampler *quilts,* in which each block is a different design.

Basic Instructions

Selecting Fabrics

Always choose tightly woven, 100% cotton fabric for appliqué. Loosely woven fabrics fray and can be more difficult to work with. The "Materials" list for each project lists the fabric amounts and colors you will need. A yardage amount, such as "¼ yard blue fabric," is for 44"-wide fabric with both selvages trimmed off. Amounts allow for shrinkage as well as variations in the cutting layout. A "scrap" is a piece of fabric no larger than a piece of typing paper (8½" x 11").

Follow our color choices if you like our combinations and have scraps in similar colors, but don't limit yourself to what we have done. Turn your imagination loose—the sky doesn't always have to be blue and trees aren't always green. We tend to use solids and quiet prints, but if you have a bolder vision, go for it! And don't forget the wrong side of fabric—it's often the perfect choice when you need a softer, faded version of a particular color. After you have assembled your fabrics, wash, dry, and press them before going on.

Supplies

In addition to the fabric required for your project, you'll need a few other supplies.

- Tracing paper, for making pattern overlays
- Masking tape, for securing the tracing paper to patterns
- Pencil (graphite or colored), for marking needle-turn appliqué templates
- Air-soluble or water-soluble pen, for marking embroidery lines
- Transfer pen or paper, for marking lettering
- Small, sharp scissors, for cutting appliqué shapes from fabric
- Optional: rotary cutter, ruler, and mat, for cutting straight-edge pieces

Appliquéing

This book teaches two appliqué techniques. The traditional needle-turn method allows you to accurately hand-appliqué even the most detailed shapes. Fusible appliqué, a more contemporary approach, uses paper-backed fusible webbing to attach the pieces.

Both methods require accuracy. Appliqué should have smooth curves and sharp points, and these are achieved with practice and patience—your most essential tools. Always cut each piece as cleanly and precisely as possible. Basic how-to's for each method follow. Some of the projects use both methods.

Needle-Turn Appliqué

Choose a long, fine needle for this technique, preferably a #11 or #12 Sharp. Work with short lengths of fine cotton thread (12" to 18"), and sew with one strand. The thread should match the appliqué fabric color as closely as possible. If you can't find an exact match, a darker, duller shade will blend better than a lighter, brighter one. Try a close shade of gray for prints with several different colors. Proceed as follows:

1. Trace each appliqué pattern directly from the book onto tracing paper, making a heavy pencil line. Cut out along the line.
2. Pin the paper pattern to the appropriate fabric, right sides up.
3. Using an air-soluble or water-soluble marker, colored pencil (we love Prismacolor pencils), or regular pencil, trace lightly around the paper shape to mark its outline on the fabric. If you use an air-soluble marker, follow the manufacturer's instructions, and mark just 1 or 2 shapes at a time so you can complete the appliquéing before the marks disappear.
4. Unpin and remove the paper pattern. Cut out the fabric shape a scant ¼" outside the marked outline.
5. Pin or baste the fabric shape to the background fabric. One trick for positioning shapes is to use a light box or window to trace either the whole pattern or several key elements onto the background as a guide. Use an air-soluble or water-soluble marker so the marks are easily removable later (always test

your marker on a scrap of the same fabric to be sure).

6. To begin appliquéing, choose an edge that is straight or gently curved and fold the seam allowance under. You want the marked outline line to fall right on the point of the fold; it should not be hidden in the seam allowance or be visible from above. Bring your knotted thread up from the wrong side of the background, catching the very edge of the fold with the tip of the needle, and then pull the thread taut. Reinsert the needle into the background at about the same place you came up. Repeat, this time coming up and catching the fold about ⅛" from your first stitch.
7. Continue in this manner, using your needle to turn under the seam allowance ½" to 1" ahead of where you are stitching and creasing the fold line with your fingers. The stitches should be tiny and even, about ⅛" apart on straight edges and closer on inside curves and sharp points. To eliminate bulk at points and corners, trim away the excess fabric just before you turn under the edge. To make inside curves and inverted points lie flat, clip the seam allowance almost to the fold line. Inverted points call for special attention because they are subject to fraying at the clip point. To prevent fraying, take smaller stitches as you near the inverted point, and make several overcast stitches at the point itself.
8. Repeat steps 1–7 for the remaining appliqué shapes, following the order given in the individual project directions. Note that you do not have to appliqué an edge that will be covered by another piece.

Fusible Appliqué

Begin by acquainting yourself with paper-backed fusible web. On the smooth side—the paper side—you can trace patterns using an ordinary pencil. On the rough side, you can feel the crystals that melt when heated by an iron.

All the patterns in this book face the right way; that is, they are printed as they appear in the finished project. Since the web is fused to the wrong side of fabric, you will need to transfer the patterns to the web in reverse. Here's what to do:

1. Trace the full pattern directly from the book onto tracing paper, making a heavy pencil line. You will use this pattern twice—first as a template for tracing pieces onto fusible web, and later as an overlay to guide the appliqué placement.
2. Turn the tracing paper pattern face down. Place the fusible web, paper side up, over the pattern. Place both pieces over a light box or hold them up to a window, then retrace the individual pattern pieces onto the paper side of the fusible web. Trace the dashed line where appropriate to complete a pattern that is partially hidden by another appliqué. If a number of pieces are to be cut from the same fabric, group them together, allowing about ¼" between them. For example, "Moon and Stars Sampler" on page 12 has gold stars, a gold sun, and a gold moon scattered over the entire piece. You would trace these patterns onto the fusible web so that they appear together. When the tracing is complete, cut out each piece, or group of pieces, about ½" beyond the outermost line.
3. Place the rough side of the marked fusible web against the wrong side of the fabric. Iron for two or three seconds, just until the web is fused to the fabric. (Fusible web is like pasta; you don't want to overcook it.) After a few experiments, you'll be able to tell how many seconds to press and the temperature setting on your iron that gives the best results. At this point, your pattern piece is still backwards from the photo and from the pattern in the book.

Fuse.

4. Lay the background fabric right side up. Place the tracing paper overlay you made in step 1 over it, also right side up. Pin along one edge only.
5. Pick up the first piece to be appliquéd, following the order given in the project directions. Cut out the shape along the pencil lines.

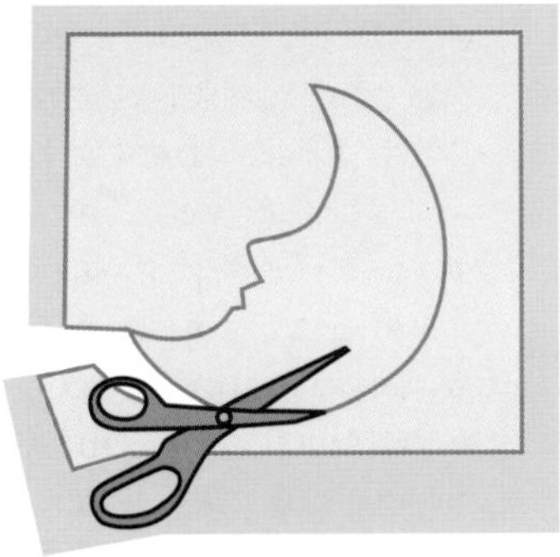

Cut out.

6. Peel off the web's paper backing.

Peel.

7. Place the appliqué right side up on the background fabric, using the pattern overlay to check the position. The piece now appears as it does in the photo and the pattern. Flip the overlay back and out of the way, and fuse the appliqué in place.

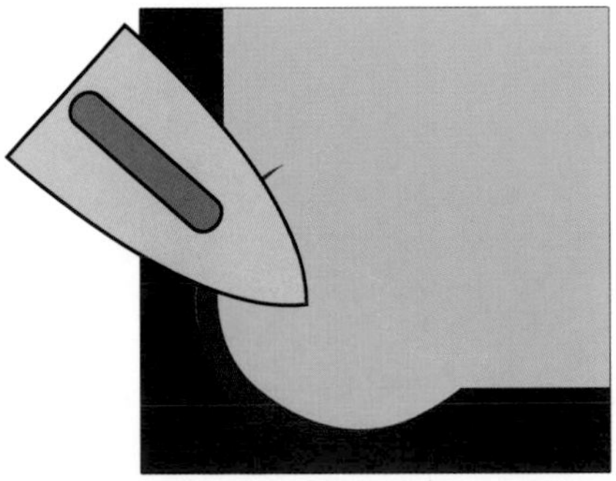

Flip over, position, and fuse to the right side of the background.

Continue to fuse each piece in turn, using the overlay to check the position. If the project instructions say, "Cut out and fuse the house, the door, and the chimney," be sure to appliqué them in that order. When the pieces have cooled, check to see that they are well adhered, especially along the edges.

Helpful Hints

- When working with small pieces or complicated designs, it's best to cut out only two or three at a time.
- Don't worry about aligning small, irregularly shaped pieces with the straight grain of the fabric. When working with solid colors, you may turn the web in any direction you want. In fact, variety in the grain positioning enhances the finished project.

Sewing Tips

Piecing

Many of the projects in this book require some machine or hand piecing. For example, the "Family Calendar" on page 35 has a pieced background, the "House Sampler" on page 27 has a pieced border, and the "Snowman Sampler" on page 40 has an interior section that is pieced.

Cut the fabric pieces that are to be joined together to the exact dimensions specified in the directions; a ¼" seam allowance is included. To prepare two pieces for joining, place them right sides together, matching edges and seams, if any, and secure with pins. Stitch with a ¼" seam, making about twelve stitches per inch. For best results, press seam allowances to one side as you go. Always press a seam before crossing it with another.

Mitering Corners

Mitered corners, with their diagonal seam lines, add a crisp finish to borders and require only a little extra effort. To ensure perfect mitered corners, follow these steps:

1. Fold each border strip in half crosswise to find the midpoint, and mark it with a pin. Also mark the midpoint of each edge of the sampler.

2. Place a border strip on the appropriate sampler edge, right sides together and midpoints matching. Pin.
3. Stitch the pieces together, starting and stopping 1/4" from the corners of the sampler; backstitch at the beginning and end to secure the stitching. Press the seam allowances toward the border. Repeat to stitch a border strip to each edge. Let the ends of the border strips hang loose.

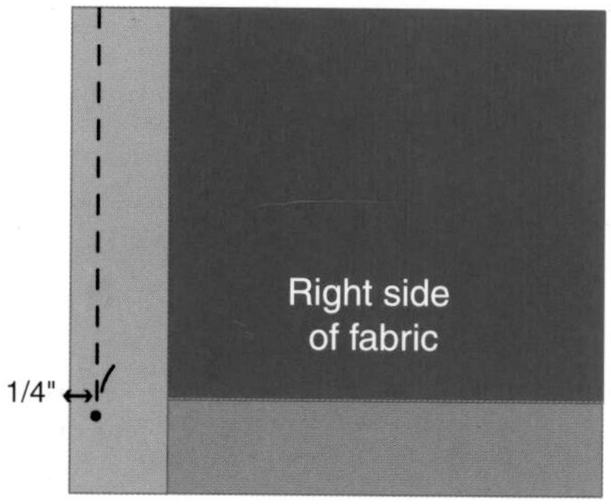

4. Fold the sampler diagonally, right side in, and align the edges of the two adjacent border strips. Using the fold line as a guide, stitch a diagonal (45-degree angle) seam. Start stitching at the end of the previous seams and take care not to catch any seam allowances in your stitching.

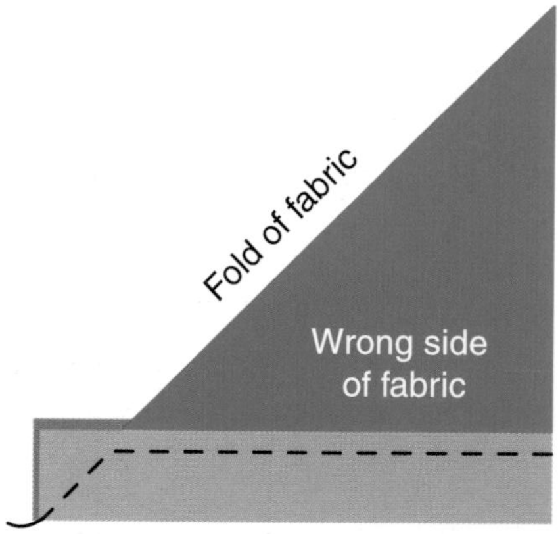

5. Unfold and check your work. The diagonal seam and the two border strip seams should meet but not overlap. Trim the seam allowance on the diagonal seam to 1/4" and press. Repeat to miter each corner.

Adding the Details

All of the projects in this book include names and dates to be written on the fabric in permanent ink or embroidered. Most projects also include other designs to be inked or embroidered, such as facial features and flower stems. In this section, we will cover our techniques for marking lettering and designs and supply detailed instructions for each embroidery stitch in the book.

Marking Lettering

There are three ways to mark lettering. One is to write words and numbers on the fabric freehand, using an air-soluble or water-soluble pen. The second is to use a light box or window to trace words and numbers onto fabric before appliquéing them to the background. The third is to use a transfer pen or paper to mark lettering after you appliqué.

We prefer the third method. Unlike writing freehand, it is precise. Unlike tracing, it allows you to plan your lettering once you know the actual finished size of the piece. Marking after appliquéing also avoids the problem of the markings rubbing off with handling.

Transferring Lettering

To transfer a word or phrase provided on the pattern, lay a sheet of tracing paper on the pattern, tape along one edge with masking tape, and trace. Skip to "Transfer Paper" or "Transfer Pens and Pencils," below, depending on the method you want to use.

To draft your own names and dates:

1. Trace around the appliqué shape or background area. To do this, lay a sheet of tracing paper on your sampler and trace the outline of the piece.

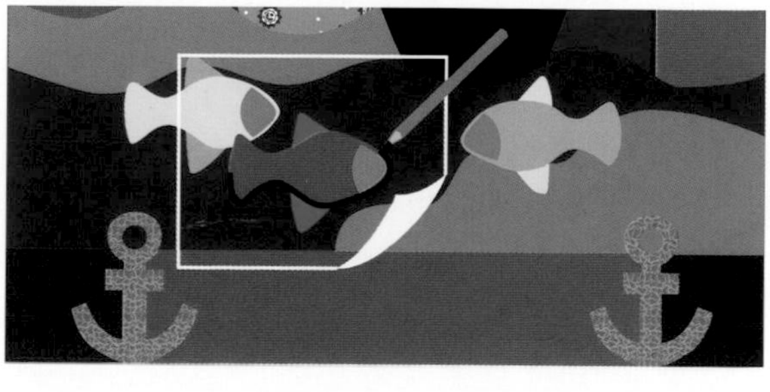

2. Decide what you want to write in the space and what style of lettering you want to use. Sample alphabets appear with most projects. You could also use your own handwriting, or trace letters and numbers from another source. Use a photocopier if you need to enlarge or reduce your alphabet.
3. Plan where each word, name, or date will appear and mark the area lightly with a pencil. Mark a straight pencil line for the letters to "sit" on.

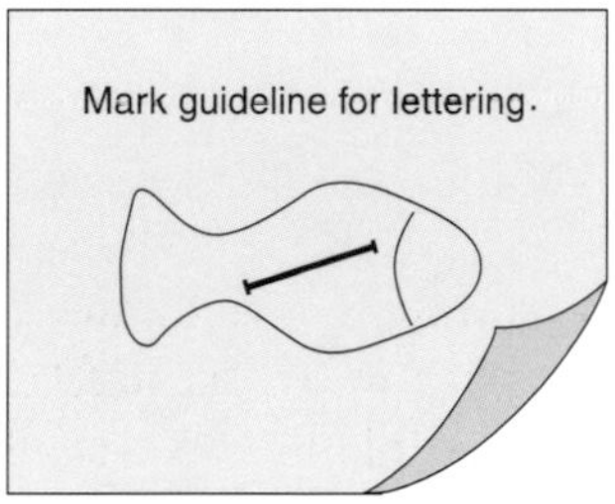

4. Lay the tracing paper pattern on your alphabet and trace each letter or number in turn.

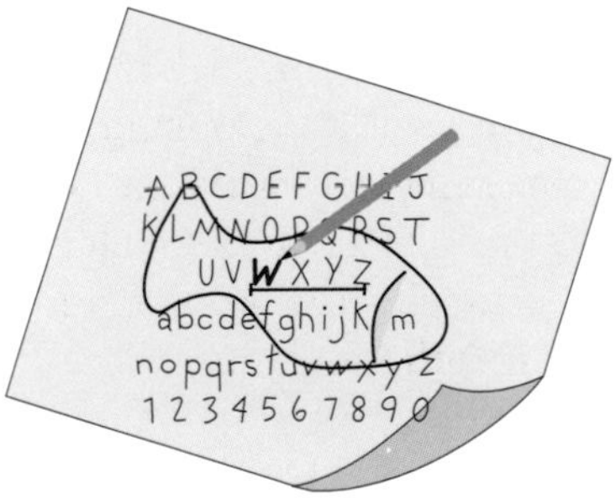

Once you have all the letters or numbers in place, it's time to transfer them onto your sampler! There are two slightly different methods for doing this.

Transfer Paper

Refer to the manufacturer's directions when using transfer paper. Details may vary from brand to brand, but this is the basic idea:

1. Lay a piece of transfer paper in a contrasting color on your appliqué shape. Place your tracing paper pattern right side up on the transfer paper with the outline matching the edges of the appliqué piece (stick pins through the tracing paper outline to check placement). Pin in place through all layers.
2. Using a ballpoint pen or pencil, re-trace all the lettering, applying just enough pressure to get the mark you desire. (Test to get a feel for this.)

Re-trace lettering to transfer paper.

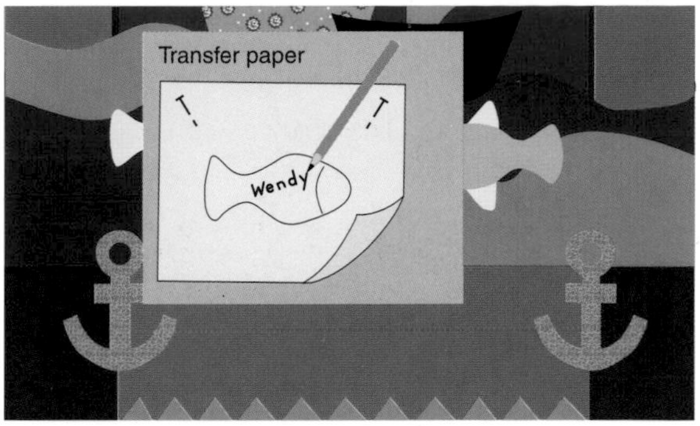

Transfer Pens and Pencils

Transfer pens and pencils leave a residue on paper that is transferred to the fabric when ironed. They come in a wide range of colors, including white for marking dark fabrics. Asymmetrical images, such as letters and numbers, need to be reversed:

1. Turn your tracing paper pattern over. Using the transfer pen or pencil, re-trace all of the lettering.

Re-trace lettering on the wrong side.

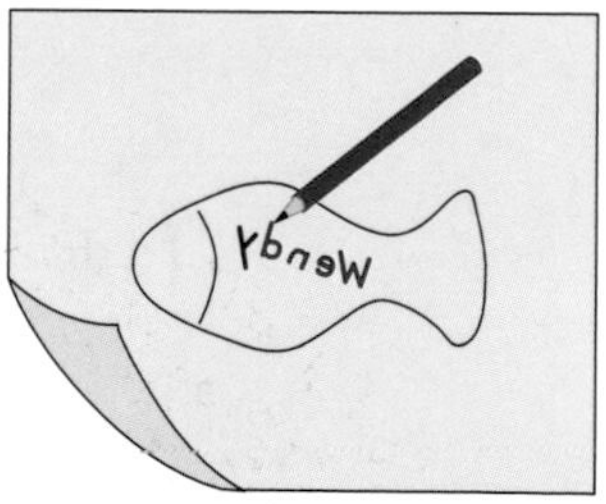

2. With the transfer side down, lay your tracing paper pattern on the appliqué shape, matching outlines. Pin.

Position and press to transfer.

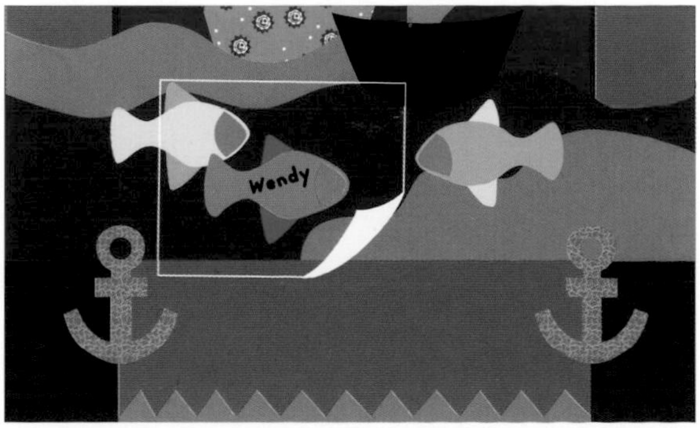

3. Follow the manufacturer's directions to iron your transfer.

Marking Details

We mark all details other than lettering freehand with an air-soluble or water-soluble pen, whether we plan to embroider or ink them. Simply refer to the pattern and photo and duplicate all lines as closely as you can, remembering you can redo them once the marks disappear or dissolve. Again, follow the manufacturer's directions and test your pen on a scrap of fabric to be sure the marks are visible and completely erasable.

If you want more precise results, you can always use one of the transfer methods described previously to mark all of the details.

Note: Air-soluble markers disappear in twenty-four to seventy-two hours. Mark only what you can embroider in that time.

Embroidering

Once a design is transferred, you are ready to begin embroidering. If you have never embroidered before, just refer to the illustrated directions below to work all of the simple stitches in this book.

Backstitch

Work this stitch from right to left. Bring the needle up at 1. Reinsert the needle at 2 and bring it up at 3. Reinsert the needle at 1 and bring it up to the left of 3. Continue in this manner.

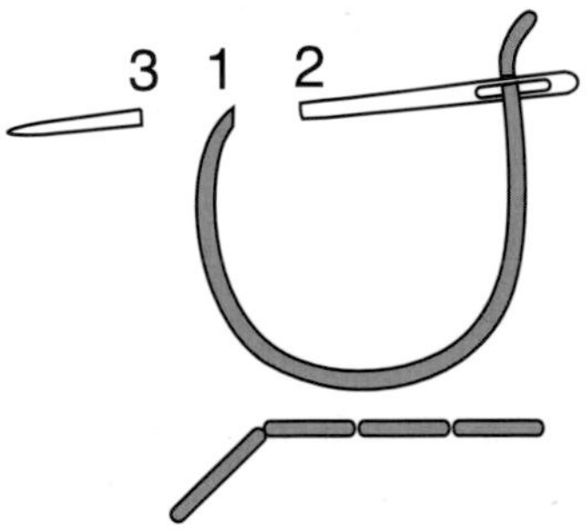

Buttonhole Stitch

Work this stitch from left to right. Bring the needle up at 1. Insert the needle at 2 and pull the thread through, leaving the section on top between 1 and 2 a bit loose. Bring the needle up at 3, to the right of 1, wrapping the previous stitch around the right side of the needle. Pull taut, then insert the needle at 4 and repeat.

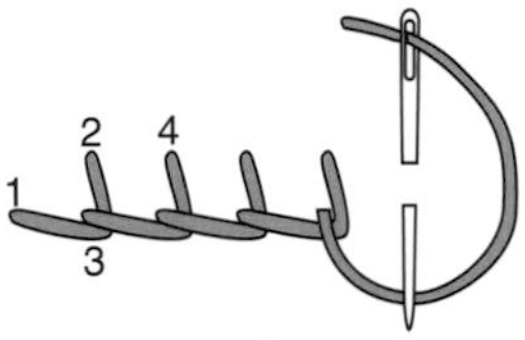

Tacking Stitch

A larger, messier version of a hand appliqué stitch used to tack down the raw edges of fused shapes.

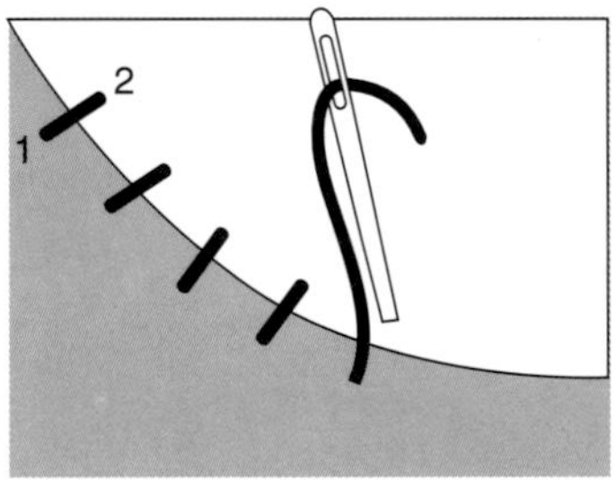

Chain Stitch

Bring the needle up at 1, hold down a small loop of thread, and insert the needle at 2. Bring the needle up at 3 and draw the loop snug but not tight. Reinsert the needle at 4, catching the first loop and holding down a new loop. Repeat to form a chain, using each new stitch to secure the previous. To end off, take a small stitch over the last loop.

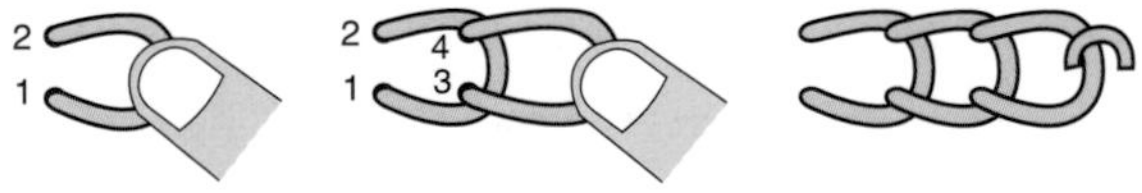

Cross-Stitch

Each cross is made of two straight stitches.

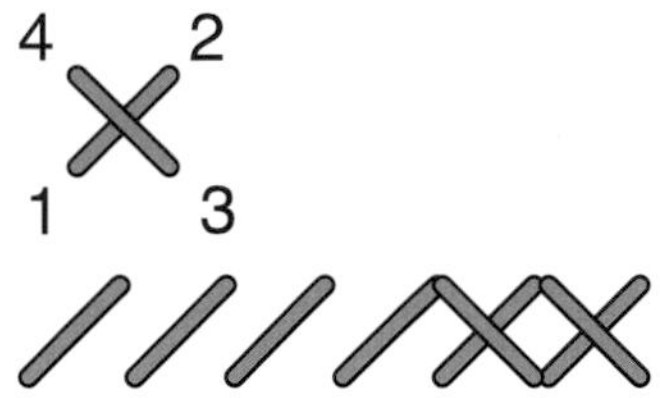

French Knot

Bring the needle up at 1 and wrap the floss once (or twice) around the shaft of the needle. Insert the needle into the fabric at 2. Change the size of your knot by varying the number of strands used or times wrapped.

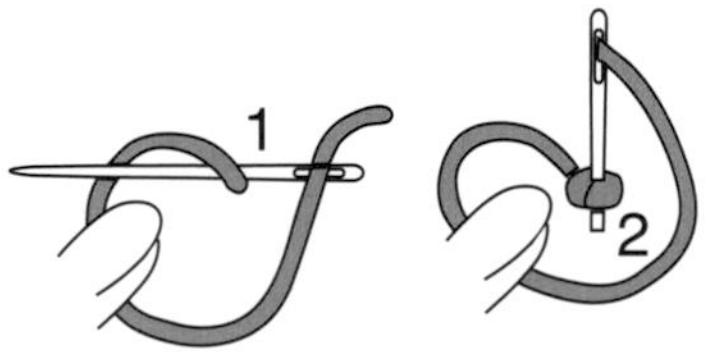

Running Stitch

This is the same stitch used for quilting. Bring the needle up at 1, then reinsert it at 2 to complete the stitch. Try to space insertion and extraction points evenly.

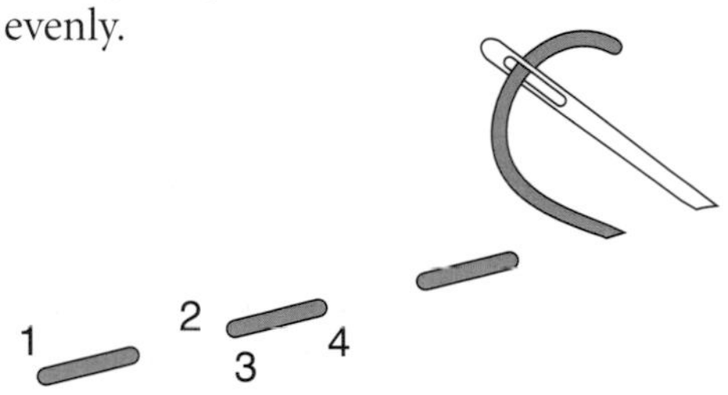

Whipped Backstitch

Backstitch to cover the markings (page 10). Then go back over the backstitches, wrapping the thread once around each stitch.

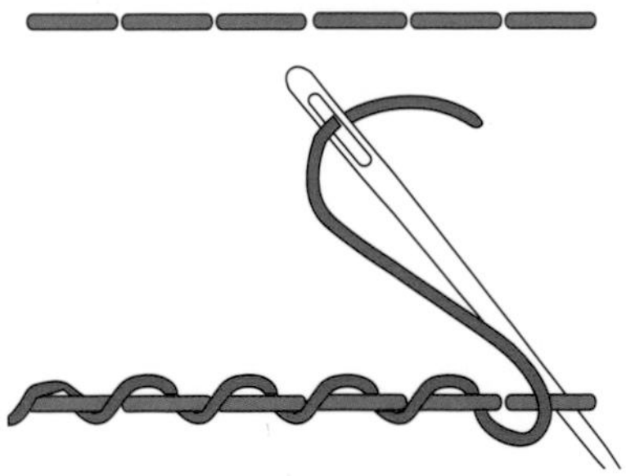

Satin Stitch

Bring the needle up at 1. Reinsert the needle at 2 and bring it up at 3, to complete the first stitch. Repeat, making parallel stitches to fill a desired area.

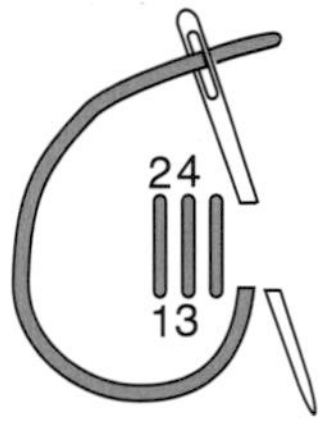

Star Stitch

Bring the needle up at 1, down at 2, up at 3, and down at 4. Continue in this manner until the entire star shape is formed.

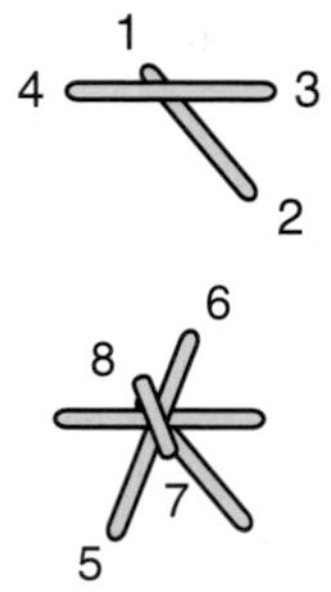

Stem Stitch

Bring the needle up at 1. Reinsert the needle at 2 and bring it up at 3 to complete the first stitch. Repeat, keeping the thread to the left of the needle, to make a line of slanted, closely spaced stitches.

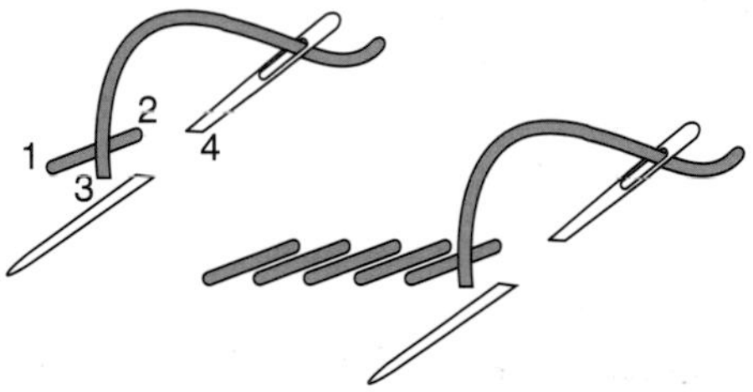

Inking

To ink over a marked detail, simply re-trace all of the lines with a permanent marking pen such as a Sharpie Ultra Fine Point. Always test your pen to be sure it doesn't bleed.

Moon and Stars Sampler

Finished size: approximately 12" x 20"

Materials

½ yard black fabric for backing
11" x 18" piece of dark gray felt for background
9" x 11" piece of blue fabric
Scraps of cotton fabric in these colors: periwinkle, pale blue, turquoise, teal, brown, rose, lavender, pale lavender, gold, yellow, and white
Dark gray thread
Embroidery floss in green, dark blue, and blue
Paper-backed fusible web
Fine-point permanent markers in navy blue, lavender, purple, green, and rose

Appliqué the Design

Note: Refer to "Fusible Appliqué" on pages 6–7.

1. Make the pattern overlay. Note that the blue pattern takes up 2 pages.
2. Turn the overlay wrong side up, and use it to trace the pattern pieces onto fusible web. Remember to group the pieces that will be cut from the same fabric, such as the gold pieces. Cut out each fusible web piece, or group of pieces, leaving a ½" margin all around.
3. Fuse each piece or group to the wrong side of the appropriate fabric.
4. Center the overlay on the gray felt background, right sides up. Pin along one edge.
5. Cut out the periwinkle piece along the marked outline. Peel off the paper backing and position the piece, fusible side down, on the gray felt, using the overlay as a guide. Flip the overlay out of the way and fuse. Cut out and fuse the yellow arc, the turquoise arc, and the gold sun, making sure the sun sits on top.

6. Cut out the blue piece; cut out and remove the interior circles. Fuse the blue piece to the gray felt background, overlapping the lower edges of the sun and arcs. Cut out and fuse the pale lavender banner. Cut out and fuse the small teal, brown, rose, and blue pieces as numbered. Cut out and fuse the white and pale blue pieces.
7. Cut out and fuse the turquoise arch. Cut out and fuse the rose, gold, and pale lavender pieces that make up the moon. Cut out and fuse the 3 lavender tails and 7 gold stars.

Add the Details

Note: Refer to "Adding the Details" on pages 8–11. Refer to the project photo and pattern for placement.

1. Using an air-soluble or water-soluble pen, draw the following embroidery designs freehand: sun's face, moon's eye and lines on cheek, and star tails. Don't bother marking the sun's rays, the running stitches along the top edge of the blue, the cross-stitches, or the lines around the double circle.
2. Using your method of choice, transfer the phrase "A Stellar Family," the word "the,"and the names you want to include (alphabets on page 14).
3. Using 2 strands of green floss, backstitch the family name. Also make a running stitch along the top edge of the blue piece.

4. Using 2 strands of dark blue floss, make small straight stitches across the sun's turquoise arc and the double circle's white border. Make a large X in each of 5 stars.
5. Using 2 strands of blue floss, backstitch the cloud lines.
6. Using a navy blue marker, ink "A Stellar Family" and add 7 small Xs to the top of the design. Ink the children's names and the faces on the sun and moon.
7. Using a lavender marker, draw an X in the center of both remaining stars.
8. Using a purple marker, ink the lines on the moon's cheek and the star tails.
9. Using a green marker, ink the parents' first names on the top banner.
10. Using a rose marker, draw straight lines across the sun's yellow arc.

Complete the Design

1. Cut out the felt background ½" beyond the fused design. Center the piece on the black fabric and hand-appliqué all around (you do not need to turn under the edge).
2. Have the piece professionally framed.

ABCDEFG
HIJKLMN
OPQRSTUV
WXYZ

ABCDEFGHIJKLMN
OPQRSTUVWXYZ

abcdefghijklmno
pqrstuvwxyz

Pattern continues on page 16

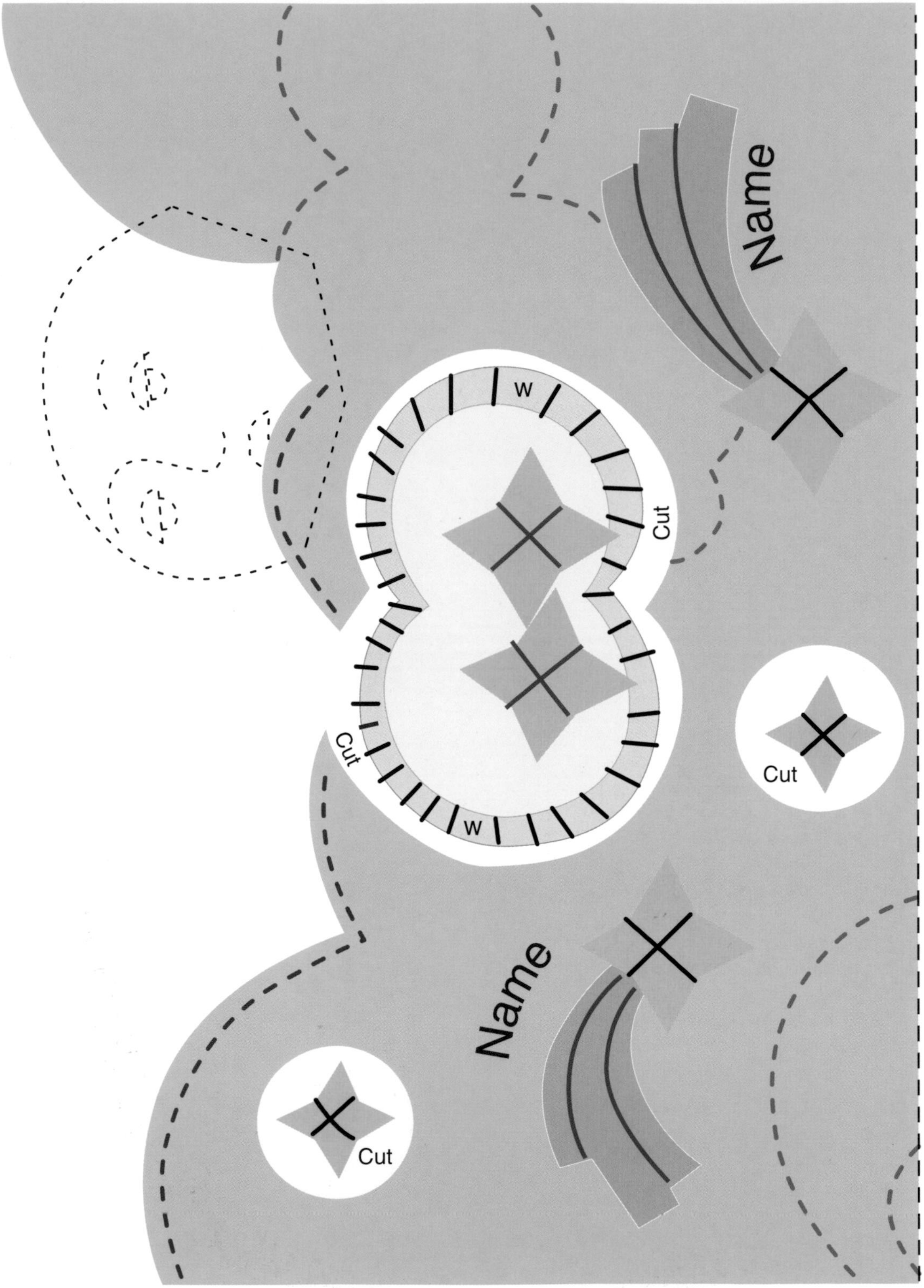

Pattern continues on page 17

Pattern continues on page 16

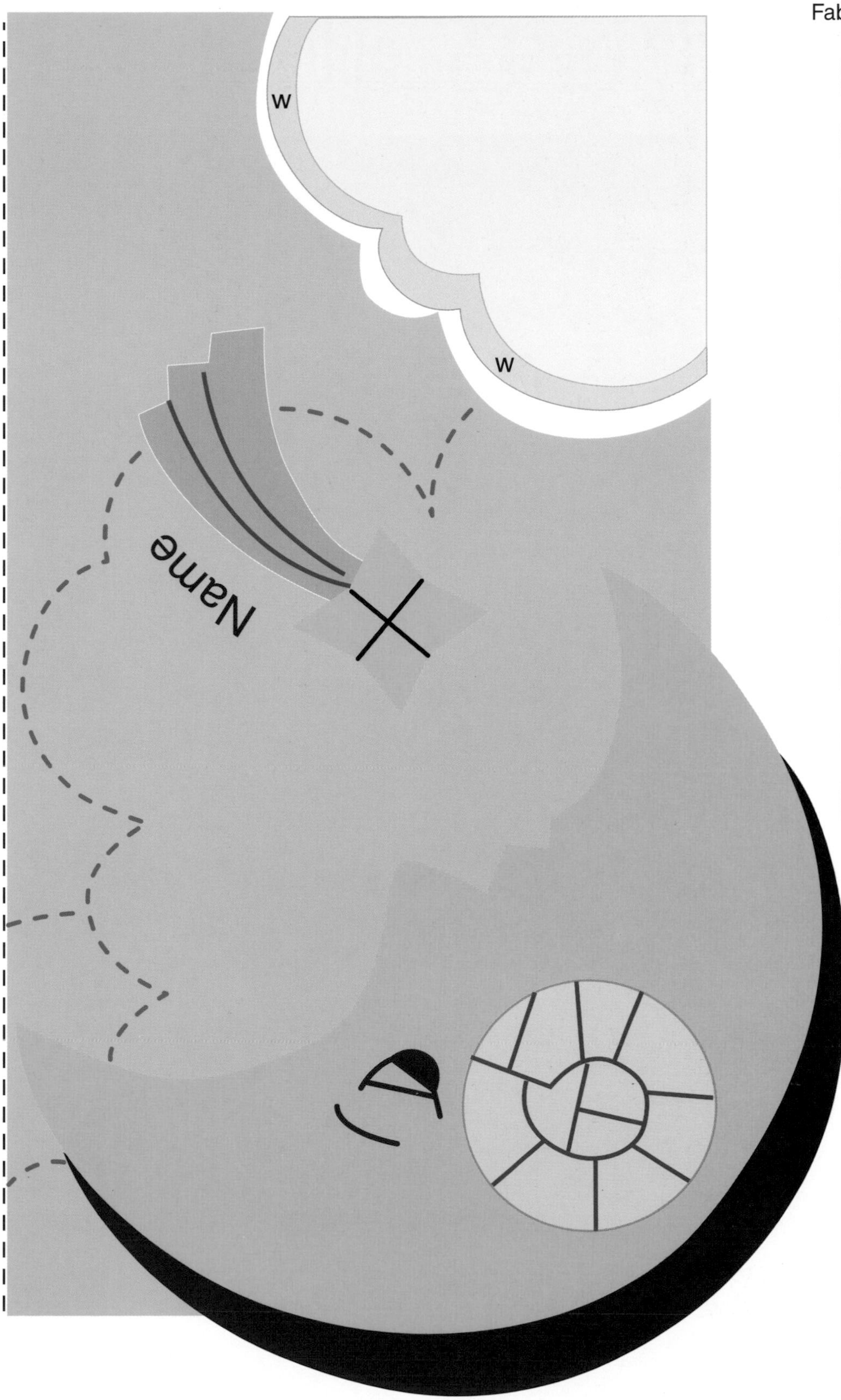

Fabric Key

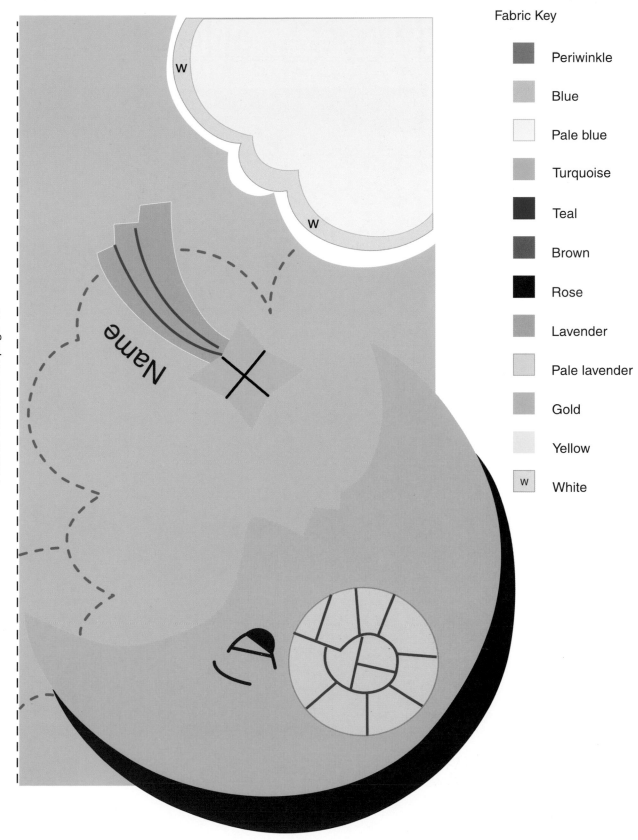

- Periwinkle
- Blue
- Pale blue
- Turquoise
- Teal
- Brown
- Rose
- Lavender
- Pale lavender
- Gold
- Yellow
- W White

Family Crest Sampler

Finished size: 11¾" x 19½"

Materials

17" x 24" piece of dark gray felt for background
6" x 12" piece of black fabric
12" x 18" piece of lavender fabric
Scraps of cotton fabric in these colors: green, olive, pale green, purple, lavender, pale lavender, gold, gold print, orange, brown, dark red, and dusty rose
Embroidery floss in white, light blue, and dark brown
Paper-backed fusible web
Black fine-point permanent marker

Appliqué the Design

Note: Refer to "Fusible Appliqué" on pages 6–7.

1. Make the pattern overlay. First, join the 3 pattern sections, then fill in the details on the lion shield.
2. Turn the overlay wrong side up and use it to trace the pattern pieces onto fusible web. Remember to group the pieces that will be cut from the same fabric. Pencil in the numbers of the small shapes that make up the stained glass sections and the lavender shield-frame sections. Cut out each fusible web piece, or group of pieces, leaving a ½" margin all around.
3. Fuse each piece or group to the wrong side of the appropriate fabric.
4. Lay a fresh piece of tracing paper on the overlay made in step 1. Trace the outer edge of the lavender shield, connecting the lines that pass under the gold banner. Cut out the shield to make a template. Lay the gray felt background right side up. Center the template on it and pin in place.

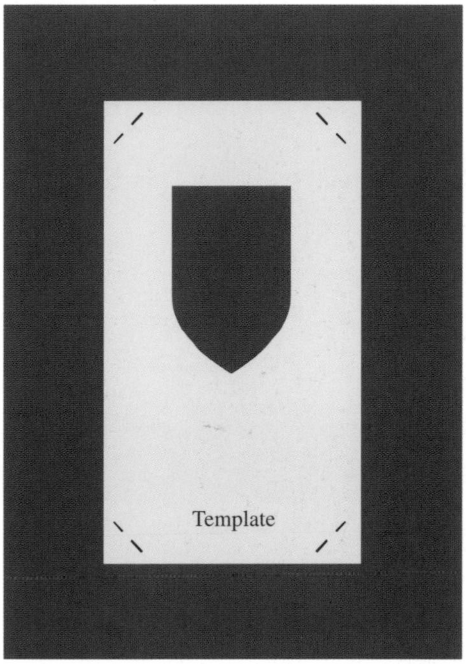

5. Center the overlay on the gray felt background, aligning the shield outline with the template. Pin along one edge.
6. Cut out both lavender shield pieces. Peel off the paper backing from one piece and position it, fusible side down, on the gray felt background. Fuse in place, remembering to flip the overlay out of the way. Repeat to fuse the second shield piece.

7. Cut out and fuse the purple body, head, and ear of the lion. Cut out and fuse the black mane and tip of the tail. Cut out and fuse the green leaf piece and the dark red flower shape.

8. Unpin and remove the template (leave the pattern overlay in place). Starting at the top left corner, cut out purple stained glass piece #1 just beyond the marked outline and fuse it to the gray felt background. One by one, cut and fuse pieces #2–#11 in the same way so that each new piece overlaps the others slightly and no background shows through. Repeat this process to fuse 13 pieces to the top right corner and 11 pieces each to the lower right and lower left corners.

9. Cut out and fuse the 4 brown pieces, 8 lavender pieces, and 2 gold-print three-quarter circles that surround the shield. Cut out and fuse the 2 dark red border pieces and the gold banner.

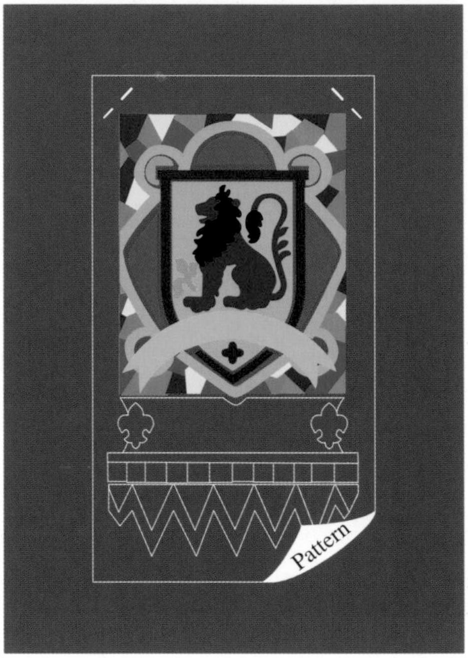

10. Cut out and fuse the large green piece, then the 2 orange fleurs-de-lis.
11. Cut out the 12 small box shapes just outside the traced lines. Fuse from left to right in this order—olive, brown, purple—overlapping the side edges slightly so no background shows through.
12. Cut out the pale lavender strip just beyond the traced lines. Fuse in place, overlapping the green piece above and the boxes below.
13. Cut out and fuse the black zigzag piece and the 7 lavender triangular pieces. Remove the pattern overlay.

14. From fusible web, cut 1 strip 3/8" x 9" and 2 strips, each 3/8" x 10 5/8". Fuse the web strips to the black fabric. Cut out each strip along the web edges and remove the paper. Fuse the shorter black strip to the top of the design, overlapping the stained-glass area. Fuse the two longer strips to each side, overlapping the black strip at the top and the stained glass along the inner edges; make sure the lower ends are even with the stained glass.

Add the Details

Note: Refer to "Adding the Details" on pages 8–11. Refer to the project photo and pattern for placement.

1. Using an air-soluble or water-soluble pen, draw the lion's features and the lines on the fleurs-de-lis freehand. Using your chosen method, transfer the word "Married" and the couple's first names and wedding date in the green area. Transfer the family name in the gold banner.
2. Using 1 strand of white floss, work the names and the word "Married" in whipped back-stitch; change to light blue floss to work the date.
3. Using 2 strands of dark brown floss, backstitch the lines on the lion's legs.
4. Using 1 strand of dark brown floss, tack the lower edge of the stained glass section and the lower edge of the boxes.
5. Using 1 strand of white floss, work a button-hole stitch along the top edge of the pale lavender strip.
6. Using the black marker, ink the family name on the gold banner. Also ink the facial features on the lion and the lines on the fleurs-de-lis. Draw lines on the leftmost edge of the dark red border.
7. Have the piece professionally framed.

Fabric Key

- Green
- Olive
- Pale green
- Black
- Purple
- Lavender
- Pale lavender
- Gold
- Gold print
- Orange
- Brown
- Dark red
- Dusty rose

A B C D E F G
H I J K L M
N O P Q R
S T U V W
X Y Z

A B C D E F G
H I J K L M
N O P Q R
S T U V W
X Y Z

a b c d e f g
h i j k l m n
o p q r s t
u v w x y z

1 2 3 4 5 6 7 8 9 0

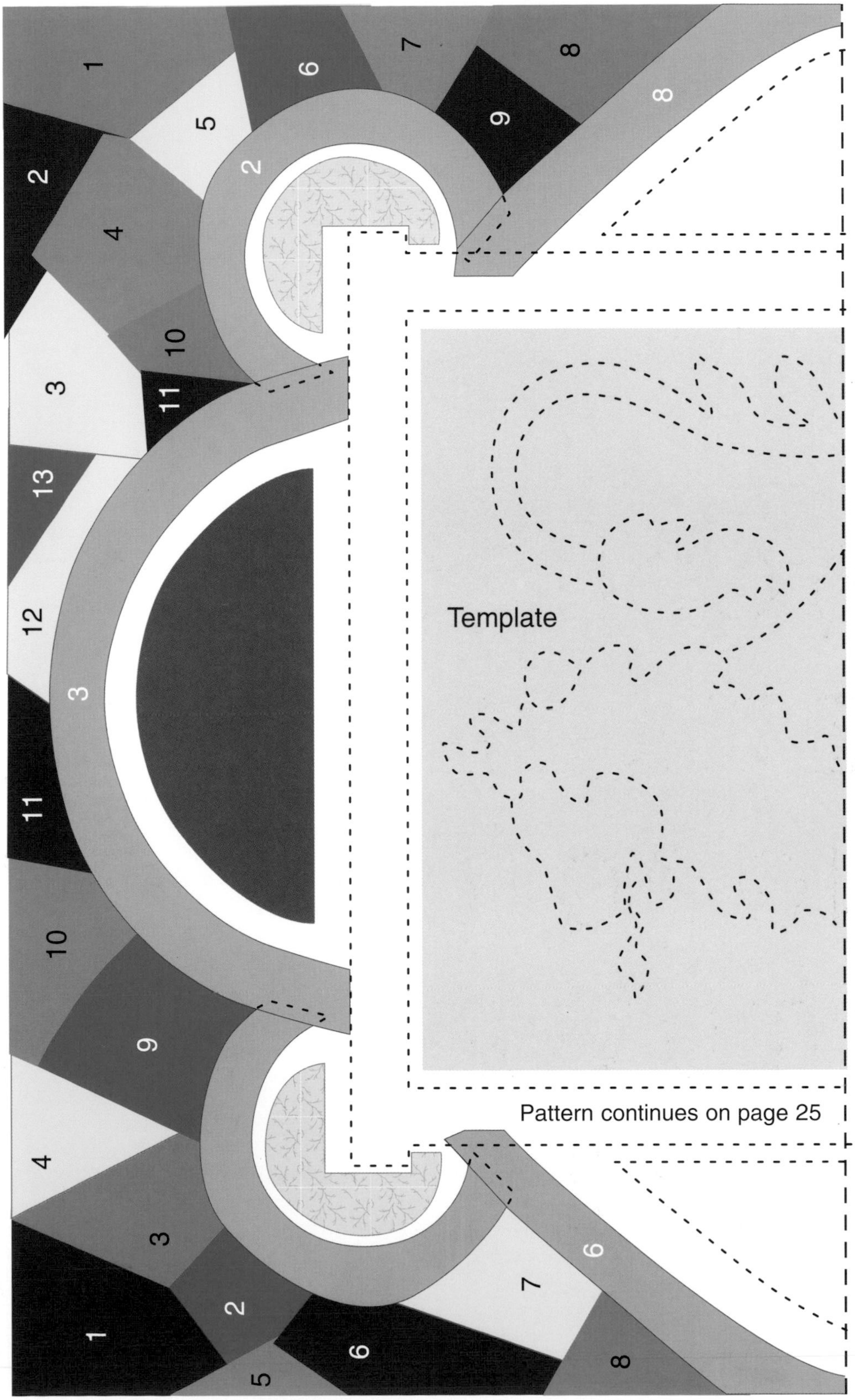

Pattern continues on page 25
Pattern continues on page 24

Pattern continues on page 23

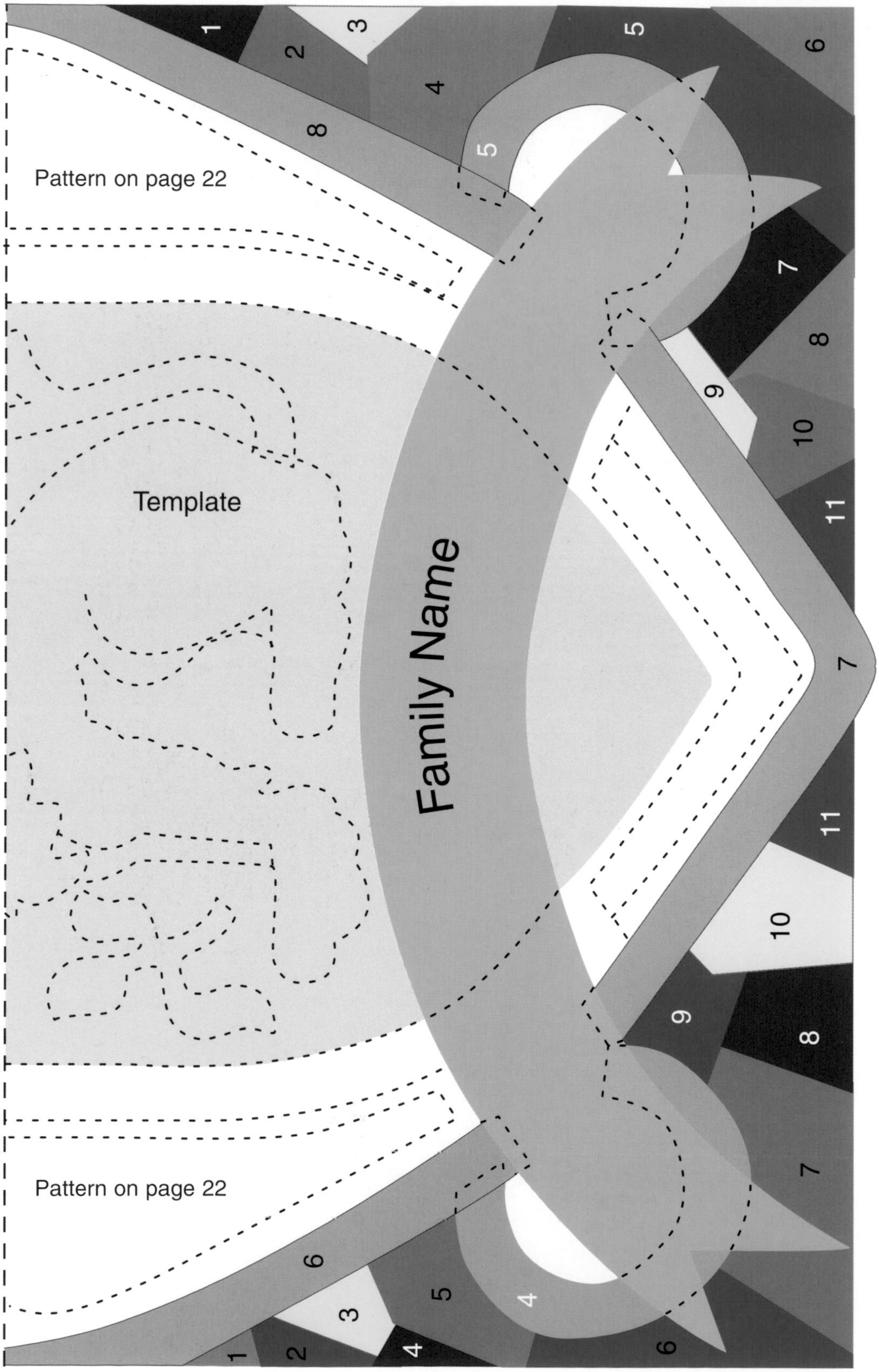

Pattern on page 24

Name & Name
Married
Date

House Sampler

Finished size: 19½" x 18"

Materials

¼ yard pale blue fabric
13" x 15" piece of white fabric for background
9" x 11" piece of dark olive fabric
6" x 14" piece of floral print fabric
Scraps of cotton fabric in these colors: navy blue, dark blue, blue, olive, pale green, green, turquoise, purple, dusty rose, lavender, dark brown, brown, brown print, tan print, gold plaid, gold, and gold print
Embroidery floss in dark brown, gray, dark gray, lavender, olive, and gold
Thread to match the following scrap fabrics: blue, olive, green, purple, lavender, dark brown, brown print, tan print, gold plaid, gold, and gold print
Paper-backed fusible web
Fine-point permanent markers in dark and medium purple

Appliqué the Design

Note: Refer to "Needle-Turn Appliqué" on pages 5–6 and "Fusible Appliqué" on pages 6–7. Refer to the project photo and pattern for placement.

1. Trace the following appliqué patterns individually onto tracing paper: 2 lavender hills, 1 tree trunk, 2 treetops, 2 roofs, 3 house walls, 1 bridge, 2 shadows under bridge, 2 lawns, and 1 stream. Cut out each pattern, pin it to the right side of the desired fabric, and lightly trace its outline. Cut out each fabric shape a scant ¼" outside the outline.
2. Trace the remaining patterns onto tracing paper (note that the dark olive border pattern must be placed on a fold). Turn the tracing paper wrong side up, and use it to trace the pattern pieces onto fusible web. Remember to group the pieces that will be cut from the same fabric, such as the navy blue windows. Cut out each fusible web piece, or group of pieces, leaving a ½" margin all around.
3. Fuse each piece or group to the wrong side of the appropriate fabric. Set these pieces aside.
4. Lay the white background piece flat, right side up, with the 13" edges at each side. Position the lavender hills on the background. Hand appliqué their top edges only.
5. Position and appliqué the 2 treetops, then the tree trunk. Appliqué the gold house wall along the edge only. Appliqué the brown-print roof around the top, left, and lower edges. Appliqué the large gold-print house wall along the left edge only. Appliqué the small wall along the right edge. Appliqué the brown roof all around.

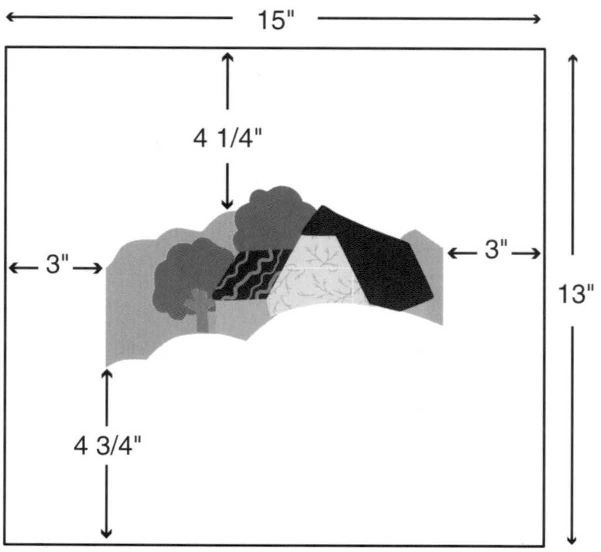

6. Position the under-bridge shadows with the navy blue piece on top. Appliqué the blue edge where it overlaps the purple piece. Appliqué the tan print bridge along the upper and lower curved edges.
7. Appliqué the left green lawn along the upper edge, the stream along the left and upper edges, and the right lawn along the curved edge. The raw edges that remain will tuck under the dark olive border.

8. Cut out the sun along the pencil line. Peel off the paper backing, then position the sun, fusible side down, above the house. Fuse in place. Cut out and fuse the chimneys, windows, and shutters. Cut out and fuse the dark olive frame, trapping the loose raw edges under it. Cut out and fuse the brown rectangle.

9. Trim the white background to 12½" wide x 11" high, centering the design from side to side and allowing 3¼" from the top of the lavender hills to the top edge.

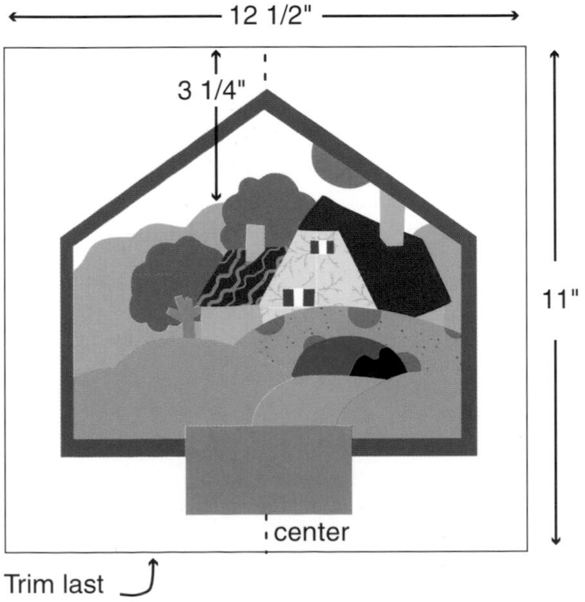

Add a Pieced Border

Note: Refer to "Piecing" on page 7.

1. Cut the following pieces:
   From the pale blue, cut:
   - 2 strips, each 3½" x 11"
   - 2 strips, each 3½" x 12½"

   From the floral print, cut:
   - 2 strips, each 1" x 11"
   - 2 strips, each 1" x 12½"

   From the gold plaid scrap, cut:
   - 4 squares, each 4" x 4"
2. Sew each 11" pale blue strip to an 11" floral print strip on the long edge. Repeat for the 12½" strips. Press. Sew a gold plaid square to each end of the 12½" units. Press.

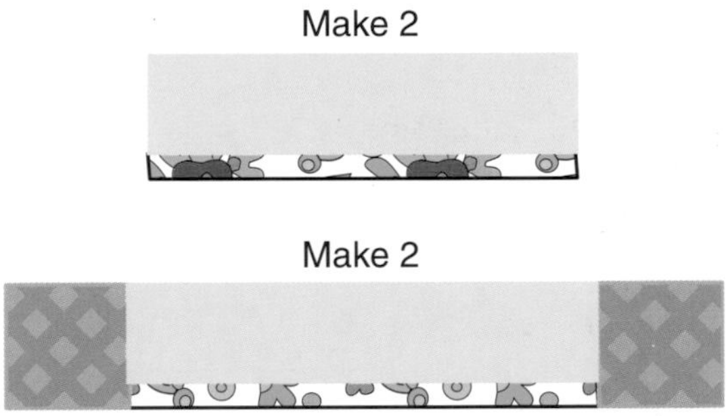

3. Sew the 11" units to the sides of the white appliquéd background so that the floral print forms an inner border. Press. Sew the longer units to the top and bottom edges in the same way, matching seams. Press.

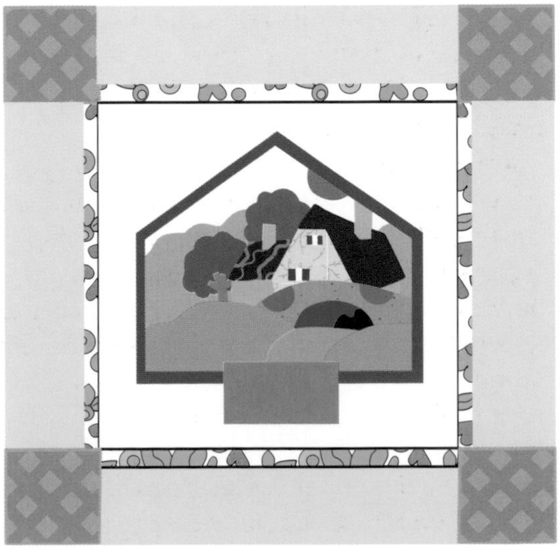

4. Cut out and fuse both turquoise pieces, then the remaining geometric shapes. Cut out and fuse the small flowers and leaves.

Add the Details

Note: Refer to "Adding the Details" on pages 8–11. Refer to the project photo and pattern for placement.

1. Using an air-soluble or water-soluble pen, draw the following embroidery lines freehand: flower centers, stream ripples, chimney lines, lines on side of gold house, lines in the lawn, and the lines to the left and right of the houses. Using your chosen method, transfer the words "Married" and "the" and the names and dates in each of the spaces indicated. Underline the family name in the brown rectangle freehand.
2. Using 1 strand of dark brown floss, work these names and dates in whipped backstitch.
3. Using 2 strands of brown floss, satin-stitch the left side of the tree trunk.
4. Using 1 strand of gray floss, sew a running stitch around the front and side of the house. Tack around the edges of the chimneys and make straight stitches down the middle to suggest brickwork.
5. Using 2 strands of gray floss, work a buttonhole stitch along the bridge's lower curved edge.
6. Using 1 strand of dark gray floss, backstitch the stream ripples. Using 2 strands, work a buttonhole stitch along the top edge of the bridge.
7. Using 1 strand of lavender floss, backstitch the lines next to the houses, to suggest a field. Make French knots on the trees.
8. Using 1 strand of olive floss, backstitch the timber framing on the left wall of the house. Using 2 strands, chain-stitch the lines in the lawn. Also work a buttonhole stitch around the inside edges of the pale blue border pieces and around the 2 light olive geometric pieces.
9. Using 2 strands of gold floss, work a buttonhole stitch around the brown rectangle.
10. Using the medium purple marker, ink the children's names at the bottom of the design.
11. Using the dark purple marker, ink the parents' names in the brown rectangle and their marriage date in the grass. Also draw the details in the small flowers.
12. Have the piece professionally framed.

Fabric Key

- Navy blue
- Blue
- Pale blue
- Dark olive
- Olive
- Pale green
- Green
- Turquoise
- Purple
- Dusty rose
- Lavender
- Dark brown
- Brown
- Brown print
- Tan print
- Gold plaid
- Gold
- Gold print
- Floral print
- White

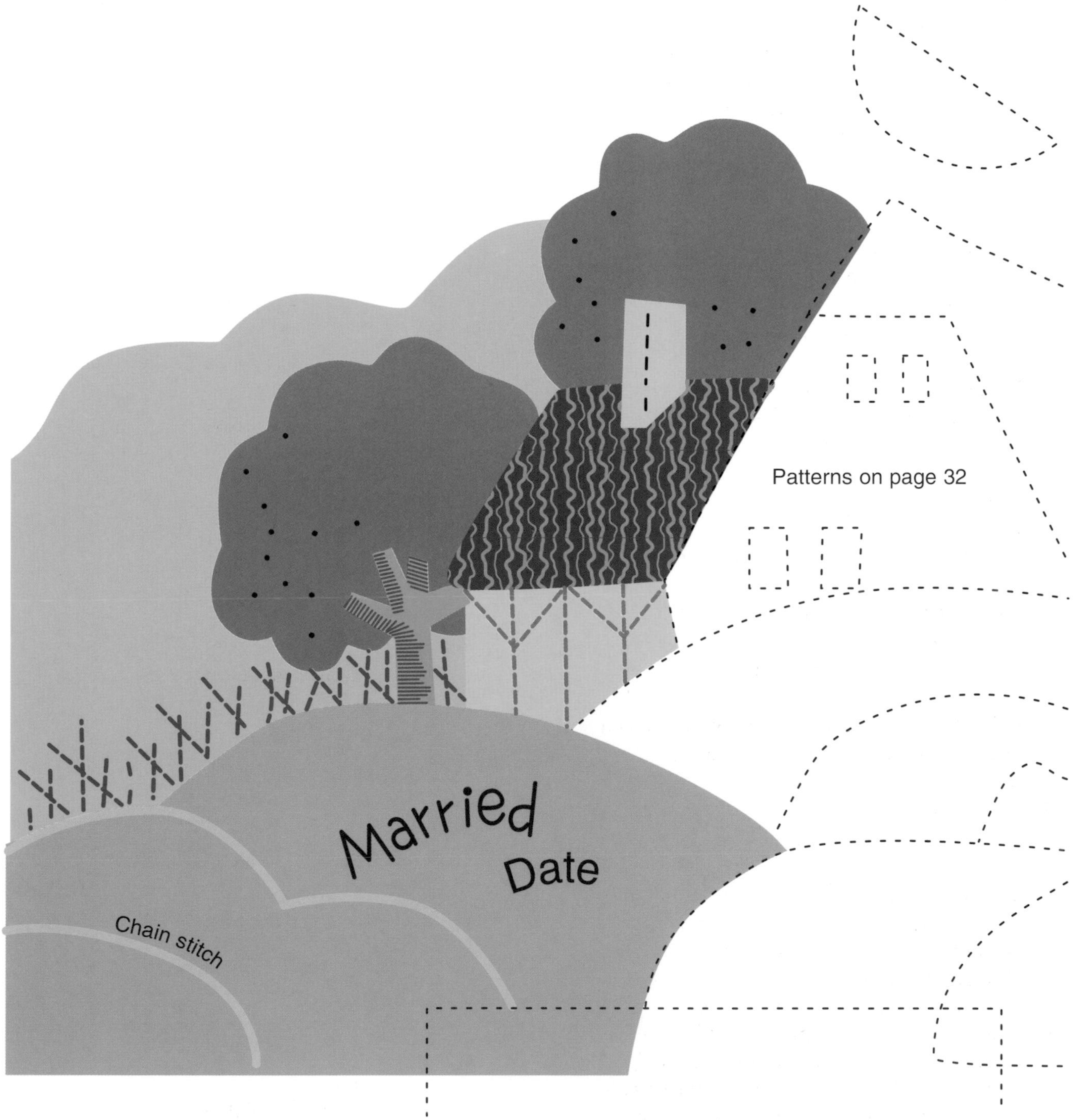
Patterns on page 32
Married
Date
Chain stitch

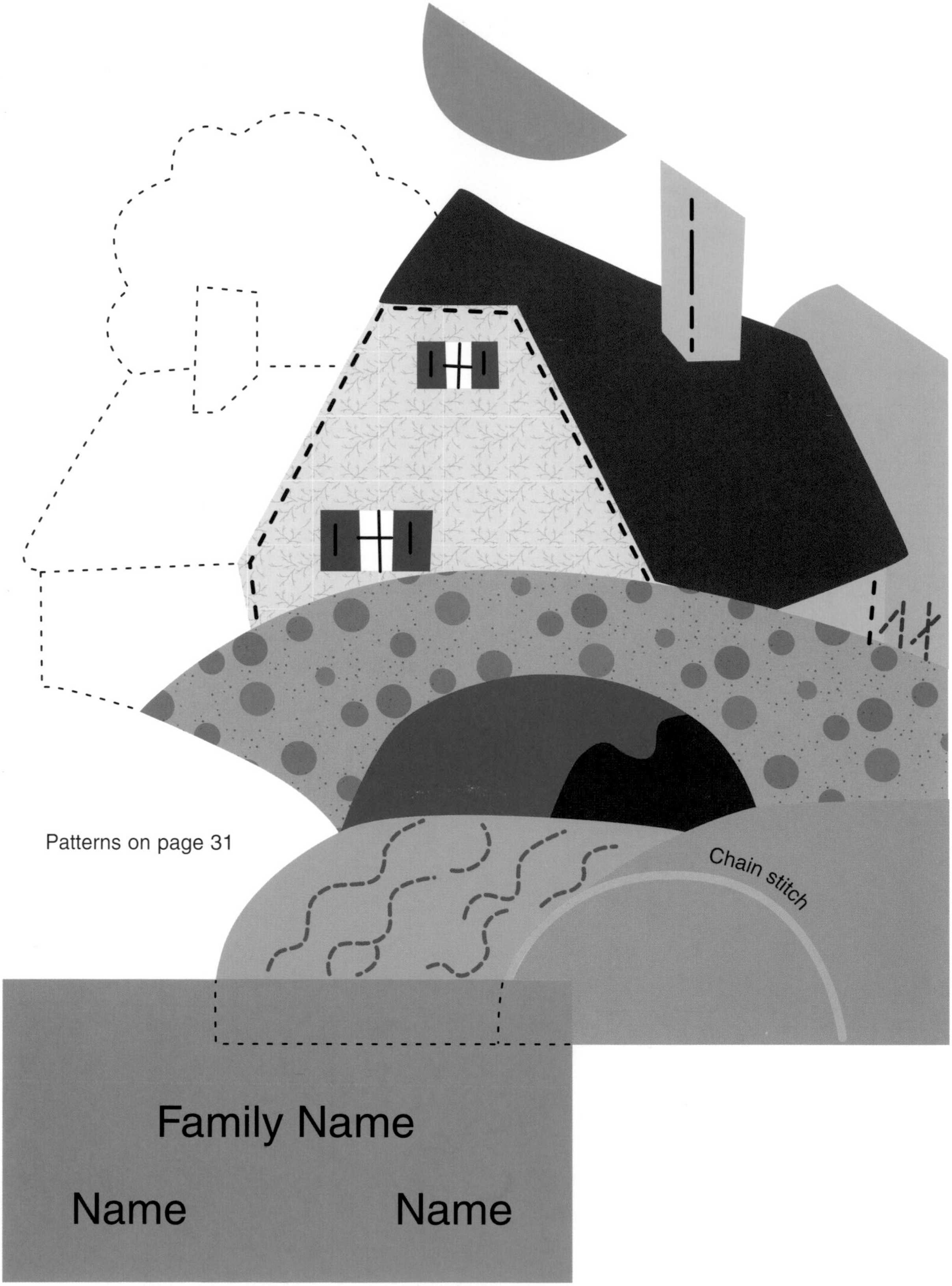

Patterns on page 31

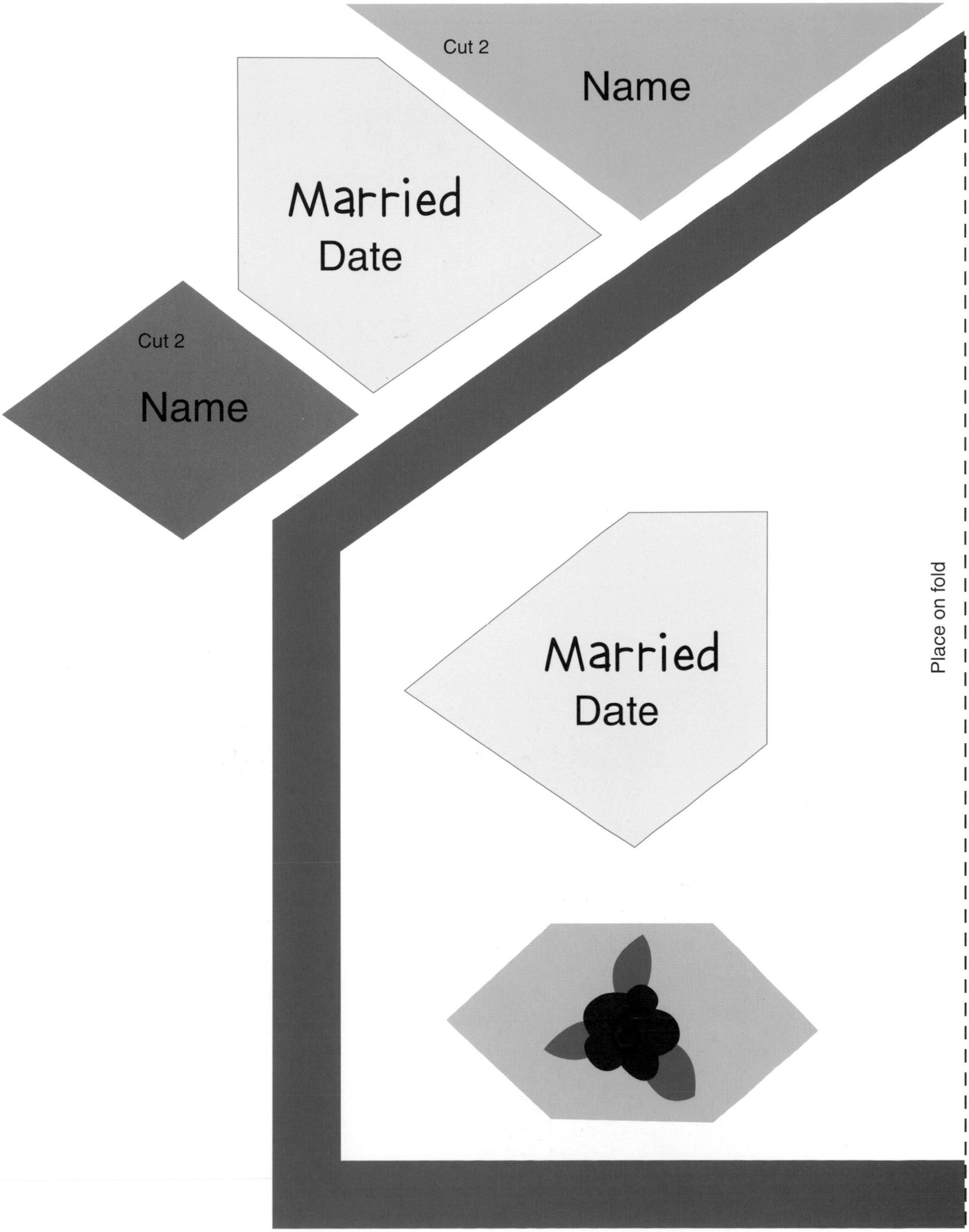
Cut 2
Name
Married
Date
Cut 2
Name
Married
Date
Place on fold

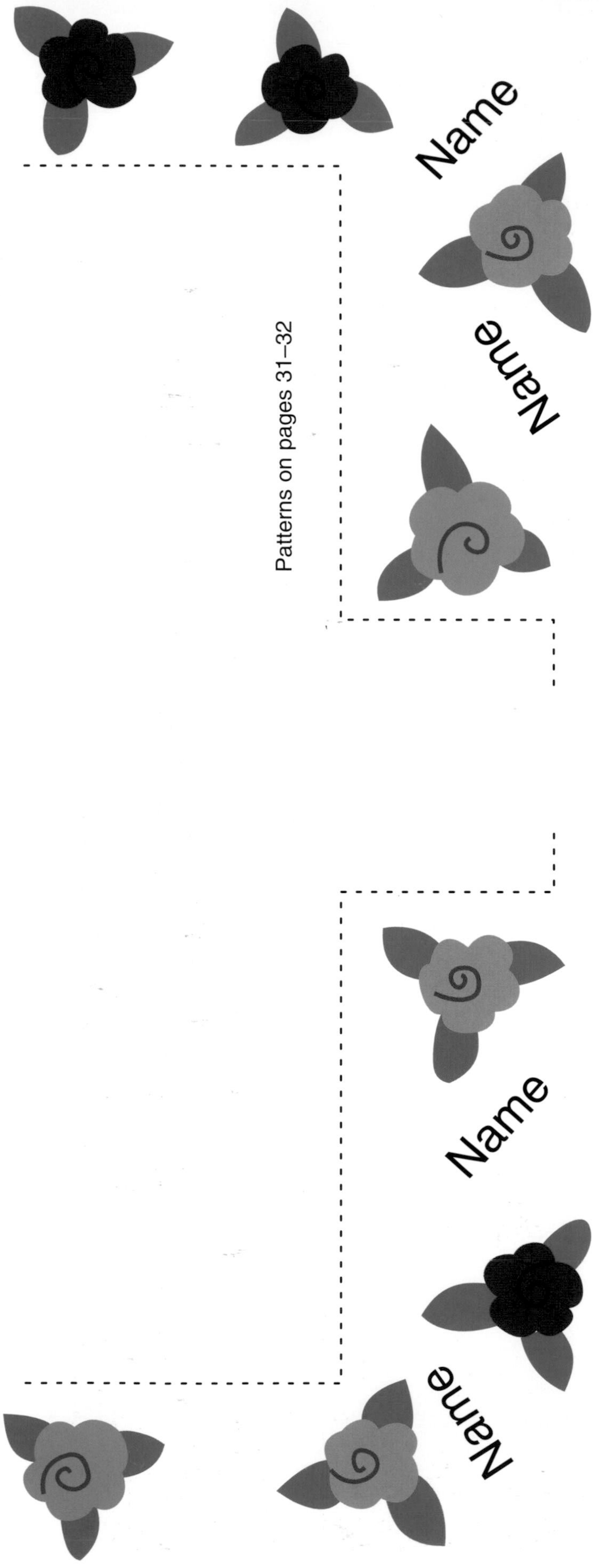

a b c d e f g h i j k l m n o
p q r s t u v w x y z
A B C D E F G H I J K L M N
O P Q R S T U V W X Y Z
1 2 3 4 5 6 7 8 9 0

A B C D E F G
H I J K L M
N O P Q R
S T U V W
X Y Z &

Family Calendar

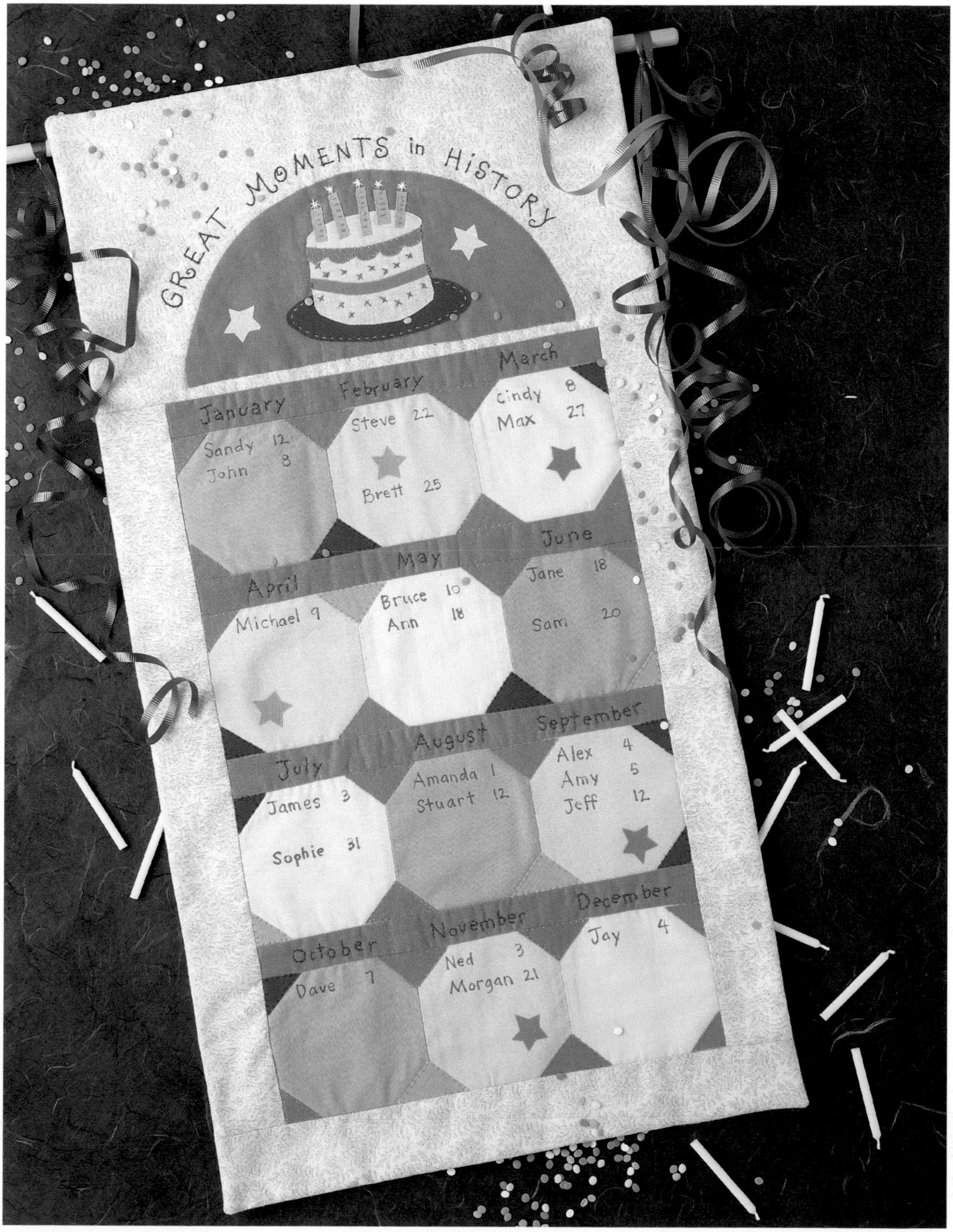

Finished size: 13" x 24"

Materials

½ yard felt for backing
1 fat quarter of green print fabric
Scraps of cotton fabric in these colors:
lavender, rose, dusty rose, pale pink, gold, yellow, turquoise, pale yellow, and blue
Lavender thread
Embroidery floss in dark blue, blue, purple, white, and gold
Paper-backed fusible web
Green fine-point permanent marker
⅜" dowel, 13" long

Assemble the Background

Note: Refer to "Piecing" on page 00.

1. Cut the following pieces:
   From the green print, cut:
   - 2 strips, each 2" x 16½"
   - 1 strip, 2" x 13¼"
   - 1 piece, 6¾" x 13¼"

   From the dusty rose scrap, cut:
   - 4 strips, each 1¼" x 10¼"

   From the gold scrap, cut:
   - 4 squares, each 3¾" x 3¾"

   From the yellow scrap, cut:
   - 4 squares, each 3¾" x 3¾"

   From the pale yellow scrap, cut:
   - 4 squares, each 3¾" x 3¾"
2. Sew the squares into 4 rows of 3 squares each, alternating the colors to match the photo. Press.

Make 4, varying color placement.

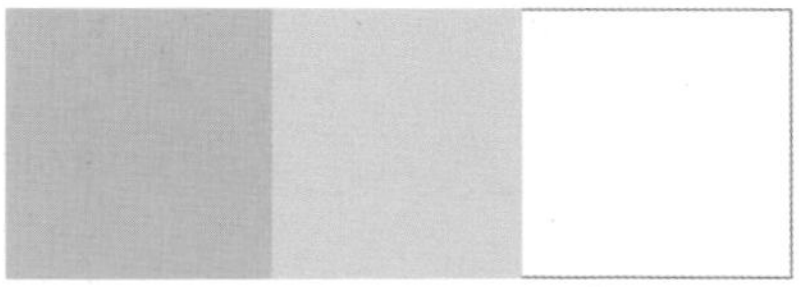

3. Sew a dusty rose strip to the top of each row. Press. Join the rows. Trim the seam allowances to a scant ¼". Press.
4. Sew the 2" x 16½" green print strips to the sides of the assembled piece. Then join the 13¼" strips to the top and bottom. Press.

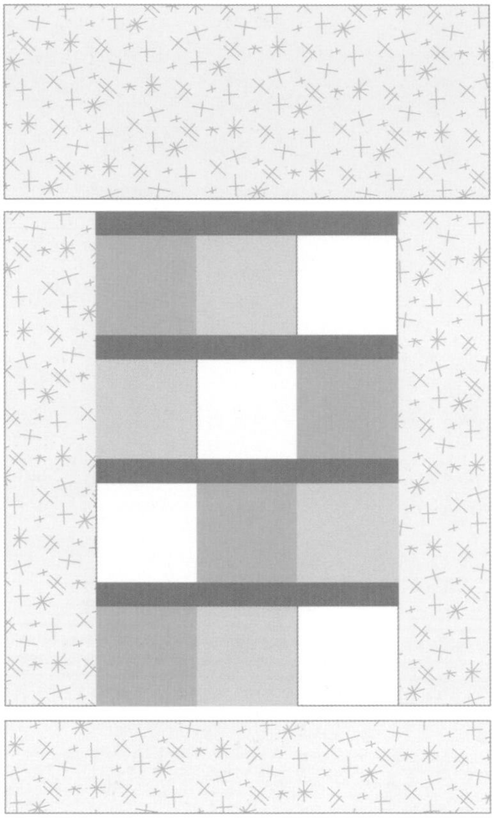

Appliqué the Design

Note: Refer to "Needle-Turn Appliqué" on pages 5–6 and "Fusible Appliqué" on pages 6–7. Refer to the project photo for placement.

1. Trace the arch pattern onto tracing paper. Cut out the pattern, pin it to the right side of the lavender fabric, and lightly trace its outline. Cut out the arch a scant ¼" outside the outline.
2. Trace the cake pattern pieces, 16 large triangles, 16 small triangles, and 7 stars directly from the book onto fusible web (these pieces are symmetrical and don't need to be reversed). Remember to group pieces that will be cut from the same fabric. Cut out each piece or group of pieces, leaving a ½" margin all around.

3. Fuse each piece or group to the wrong side of the appropriate fabric. For the triangles, use lavender, rose, dusty rose, and turquoise. For the stars, use rose, pale yellow, and blue.
4. Position the lavender arch on the pieced background, centering it 1/4" above the top dusty rose strip. Appliqué all the edges.
5. Cut out the cake plate along the marked outline. Peel off the paper backing, and position the piece, fusible side down, on the lavender arch, 1/4" above the lower edge and centered from side to side. Fuse in place. Cut and fuse the main cake piece, the 2 frosting pieces, the cake top, and candles.
6. Cut and fuse the 16 large and 16 small triangles to the corners of the 12 squares (the small triangles will cover one corner each and the large triangles will cover two corners each). Be sure to mix up the colors as shown.

7. Cut out and fuse the stars in place.

Add the Details

Note: Refer to "Adding the Details" on pages 8–11. Refer to the project photo and pattern for placement.

1. Using your chosen method, transfer the words "Great Moments in History," the names of the months, and your family names and birth dates in the appropriate places.
2. Using 2 strands of dark blue floss, backstitch "Great Moments...."
3. Using 2 strands of blue floss, cross-stitch the Xs on the cake.
4. Using 2 strands of purple floss, backstitch the names of the months.
5. Using 2 strands of white floss, make a star stitch above each candle.
6. Using 2 strands of gold floss, work a running stitch around the edge of the cake plate and straight stitches on the candles. Also tack around the edge of lavender icing.
7. Using the green marker, ink the names and birth dates on the calendar.

Finish the Wall Hanging

1. From the felt, cut a piece 14" x 25" or slightly larger than the assembled sampler.
2. Layer the felt and the sampler right sides together. Sew around the outside edges of the sampler, leaving a 3" opening for turning. Trim the felt close to the stitching and trim the corners diagonally to eliminate bulk. Turn right side out and slip-stitch the opening closed. Press.
3. To make a hanging sleeve, cut a 2" x 13" strip of fabric. Fold the short raw edges under twice and hem. Fold the strip in half lengthwise, right sides together, and sew the long edges together with a 1/4" seam. Turn the sleeve right side out. Pin the sleeve to the top wrong side of the wall hanging, and slip-stitch the top edge. Insert the dowel. Tack the bottom edge of the sleeve to the wall hanging back.

January February March

April May June

July August September

October November December

ABCDEFG
HIJKLM
NOPQR
STUVW
XYZ

abcdefg
hijklmn
opqrst
uvwxyz

1234567890

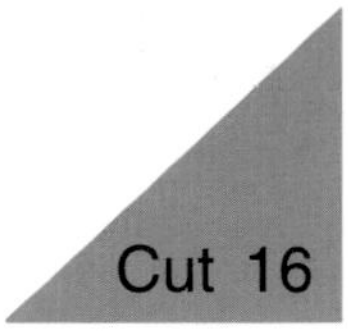

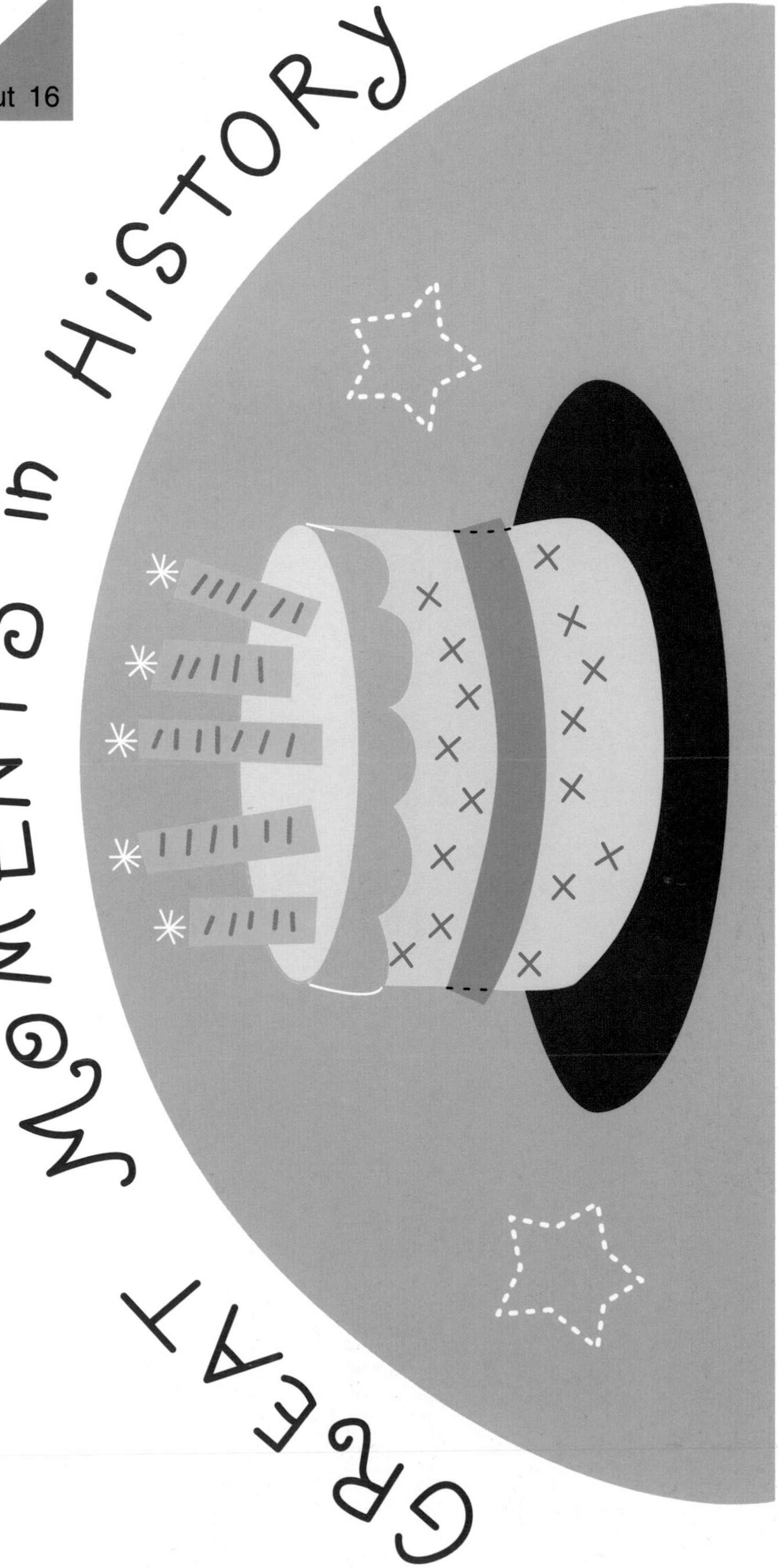

Fabric Key

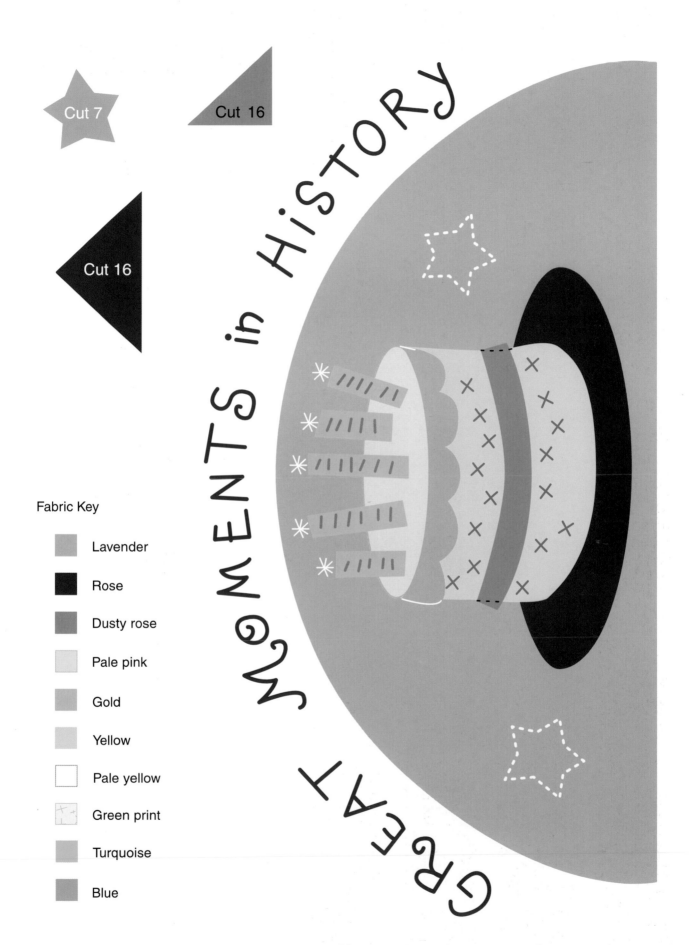

- Lavender
- Rose
- Dusty rose
- Pale pink
- Gold
- Yellow
- Pale yellow
- Green print
- Turquoise
- Blue

Snowman Sampler

Finished size: 16½" x 22"

Materials

⅝ yard fabric for backing
½ yard navy blue fabric
1 fat quarter of purple fabric for binding
10" x 12" piece of blue fabric
10" x 12" piece of light blue fabric
Scraps of cotton fabric in these colors: white, turquoise, green, olive, lavender, dark red, dark pink, dusty rose, and gold
20" x 26" piece of polyester fleece
Navy blue thread
White quilting thread
Embroidery floss in black, dark blue, medium blue, olive, orange, burnt orange, and white
Thread or embroidery floss to match these fabrics: dark red, light blue
Paper-backed fusible web
⅜" dowel, 17" long

Prepare the Border

1. Cut the following pieces:
   From the navy, cut:
   - 2 pieces, each 4½" x 12"
   - 1 piece, 8½" x 10"
   - 1 piece, 4½" x 8½"
   - 1 piece, 7" x 16½"

   From the blue, cut:
   - 2 squares, each 4½" x 4½"
2. Trace the blue/lavender striped border onto tracing paper. Mark each short stripe B1, L1, B2, L2, etc. Cut along the lines.

Trace and label.

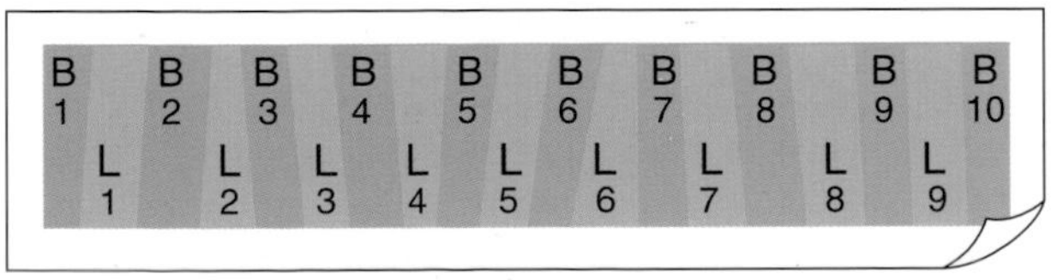

3. Pin the B patterns to the blue fabric, right sides up, at least ½" apart. Trace around each shape and cut out, adding ¼" all around, or use your rotary cutter and ruler to measure and cut in one step. Do not unpin the patterns until you are ready to sew them. Repeat with the L patterns and the lavender fabric.

Pin to fabric and cut out.

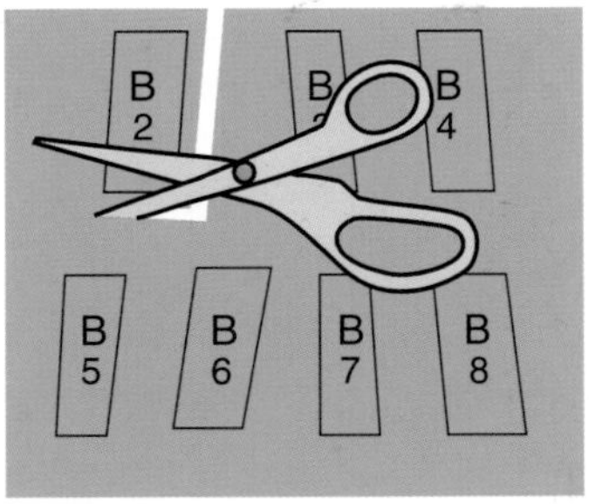

4. Sew B1 to L1, right sides together, making a ¼" seam. Now sew B2 to L1. Continue to join each piece in turn until the finished strip measures 2" x 8½". Press all the seam allowances to one side. Set this blue/lavender strip aside.

Appliqué the Design

Note: Refer to "Needle-Turn Appliqué" on pages 5–6 and "Fusible Appliqué" on pages 6–7. Refer to the project photo and pattern for placement.

1. For the background, trim your light blue f abric to 8½" x 10½".
2. Trace the navy blue snowman background onto tracing paper and cut along the drawn lines. Position the pattern on the 8½" x 10½" navy piece, trace around it, and cut it out, adding a scant ¼" seam allowance.

3. Position the navy snowman background on the light blue piece so that the lower right corners and lower edges match up.
4. Hand appliqué the upper and side edges of the navy snowman background with the navy thread. (The lower edge will be caught in a seam.) Make the pattern overlay (pages 45–46).

5. Turn the overlay wrong side up and use it to trace the remaining pattern pieces onto fusible web. Working from the patterns in the book, trace the zigzag borders, snowflake rectangle and frame, and quilt block shapes onto fusible web. These patterns don't need to be reversed. Trace the red and blue mittens and cuffs, then turn the tracing paper over and re-trace on the back, then trace these reversed patterns onto fusible web. Remember to group pieces that will be cut from the same fabric, such as the white snowflakes. Cut out each fusible web piece, or group of pieces, leaving a ½" margin all around.
6. Fuse each piece or group to the wrong side of the appropriate fabric.
7. Position the overlay on the 8½" x 10½" light blue piece, right sides up. Pin the overlay to the fabric along one edge.
8. Cut out the snowman couple along the marked outline. Peel off the paper backing and position, fusible side down, on the navy snowman background, using the overlay as a guide. Flip the overlay out of the way and fuse. Cut out and fuse the 2 turquoise pieces, his blue hat and feather, and her dusty rose hat. Cut out and fuse her gold cuff trims, the red heart, and the green and lavender mittens.

9. Cut out and fuse the 2 lavender pieces at the top corners. Remove the overlay.

10. Sew the blue/lavender strip to the bottom edge, right sides together, making a ¼" seam. Press. Cut and fuse the gold rectangle and its navy blue frame over the seam.

Assemble the Background

Refer to "Piecing" on page 7.

1. Sew a 4½" blue square to each end of the 4½" x 8½" navy blue piece. Press toward the navy blue.
2. Sew a 4½" x 12" navy blue piece to each side of the appliquéd piece. Press toward the border. Sew the navy blue/blue unit from step 1 to the top of the piece, aligning edges and matching seams. Sew the 7" x 16½" piece to the bottom of the assembled piece. Press toward the borders.

3. Cut out and fuse 3 olive zigzag borders to fit around the top and side edges of the snowman panel. Let ¼" of navy blue show along the inside edges (see photo).
4. Cut out and fuse the white snowflakes and the quilt block shapes. Cut out and fuse the red and blue mittens and their cuffs.

Add the Details

Note: Refer to "Adding the Details" on pages 8–11. Refer to the project photo and pattern for placement.

1. Using an air-soluble or water-soluble pen, draw the embroidery lines freehand. Using your chosen method, transfer the couples' and children's names and the dates in each of the spaces indicated.
2. Using 2 strands of black floss, backstitch the names in the gold rectangle and the snowflakes, the date in the heart, and his mouth and her nose; cross-stitch their eyes so each stitch reads as a + instead of an X. Make 2 French knots on his front for buttons.
3. Using 2 strands of dark blue floss, backstitch lines to define the arms, hats, flower, and lavender mittens. Sew a running stitch in the center of the feather. Backstitch the names in the blue mittens.

4. Using 2 strands of medium blue floss, stem-stitch the strings for the blue mittens. Using 2 strands of olive floss, stem-stitch the remaining mitten strings.
5. Using 2 strands of orange floss, satin-stitch his carrot nose.
6. Using 2 strands of burnt orange floss, backstitch her mouth.
7. Using 2 strands of white floss, backstitch the names in the dark red mittens and the names above the mitten strings.
8. Using matching thread or floss (1 strand), tack around the following shapes: olive zigzags, snowflakes, heart, navy frame, and red and blue mittens.

Finish the Wall Hanging

Note: Refer to the project photo and pattern for placement.

1. Using an air-soluble or water-soluble pen, mark horizontal and vertical quilting lines 1" apart on the navy blue border. Mark quilting lines ¼" to ½" apart echoing the outside corners of the blue squares.
2. For the backing, cut a 20" x 26" piece of fabric. Lay it flat, wrong side up, and lay the fleece on top. Center the sampler, right side up, on the fleece. Baste.
3. Using white thread, quilt all the lines marked in step 1. Quilt around the snow couple, the 2 bottom sets of mittens, the stars, the snowflakes, the upper edge of the light blue background, and the olive zigzag edges. Trim the fleece and backing to match the quilt top.
4. From the purple fabric, cut 3"-wide bias strips, piecing as needed to yield 2¼ yards. Fold the bias strip in half lengthwise and press. Pin the strip to the right side of the quilted piece, raw edges matching. Machine-stitch all around, gently rounding each corner. To complete the binding, fold the strip to the wrong side and slip-stitch in place.
5. To make a hanging sleeve, cut a 2" x 16" strip of fabric. Fold the short raw edges under twice and hem. Fold the strip in half lengthwise, right sides together, and sew the long edges together with ¼" seam. Turn the sleeve right side out. Pin the sleeve to the top wrong side of the wall hanging, and slipstitch the top edge. Insert the dowel. Tack the bottom edge of the sleeve to the wall hanging back.

Fabric Key

- Navy blue
- Blue
- Light blue
- White
- Turquoise
- Green
- Olive green
- Lavender
- Red
- Dark pink
- Dusty rose
- Gold

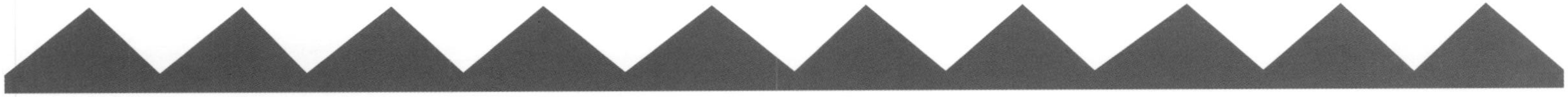

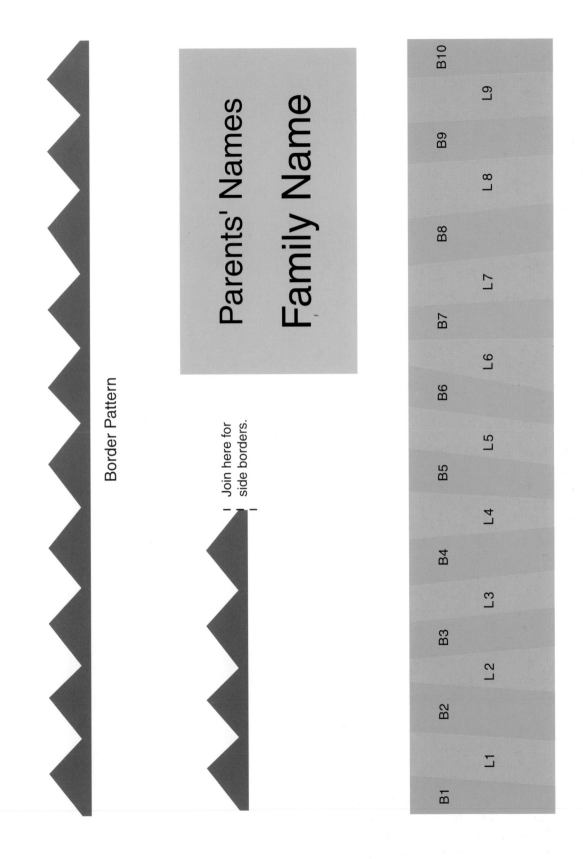

Border Pattern

Join here for
side borders.

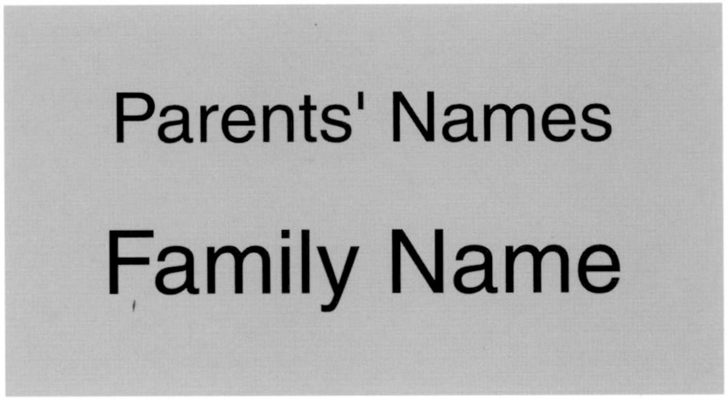

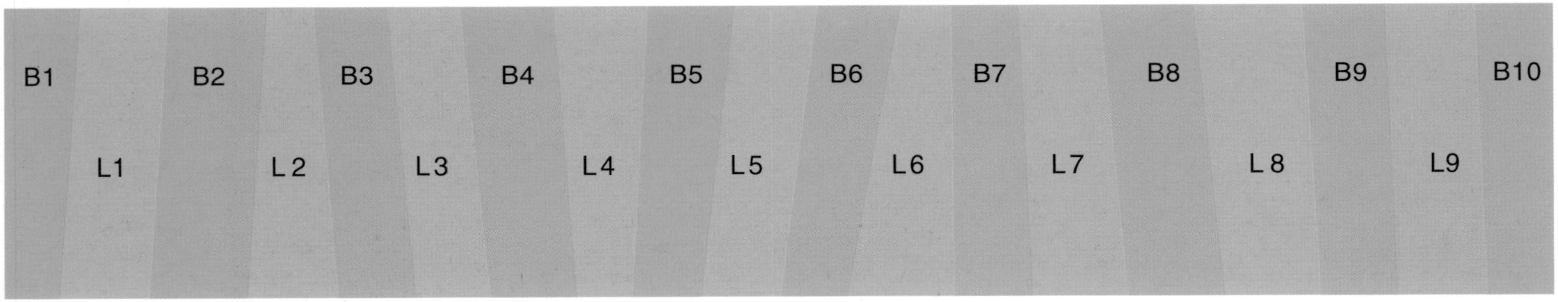

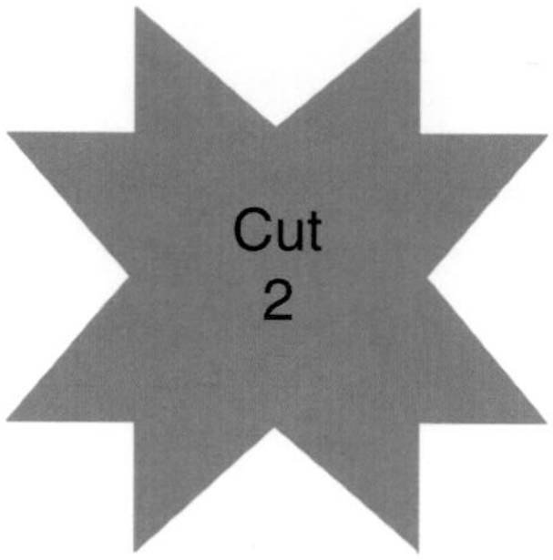
Cut
2

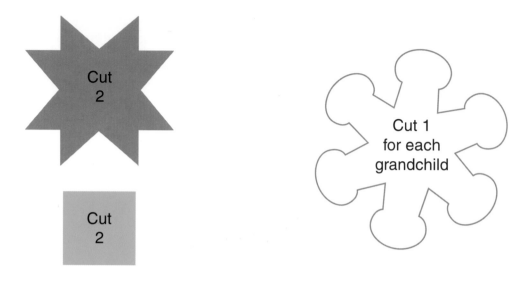

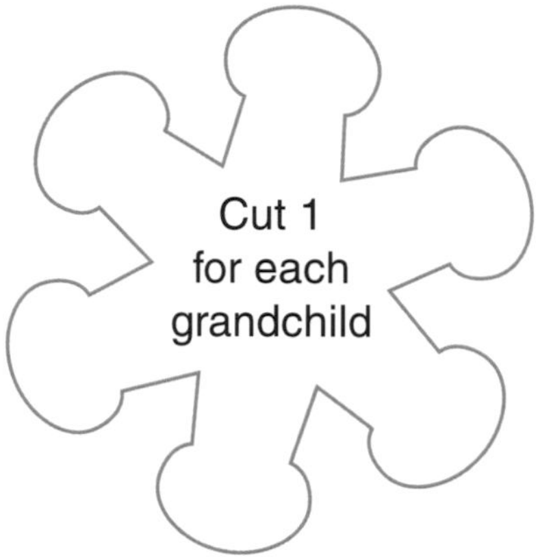
Cut 1
for each
grandchild

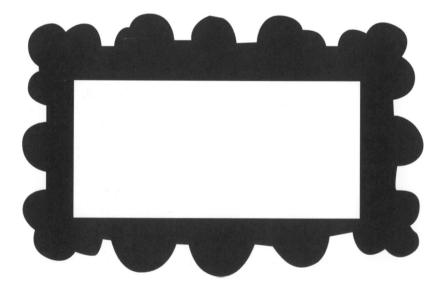

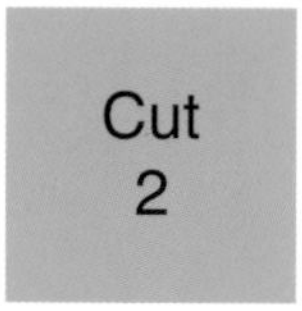
Cut
2

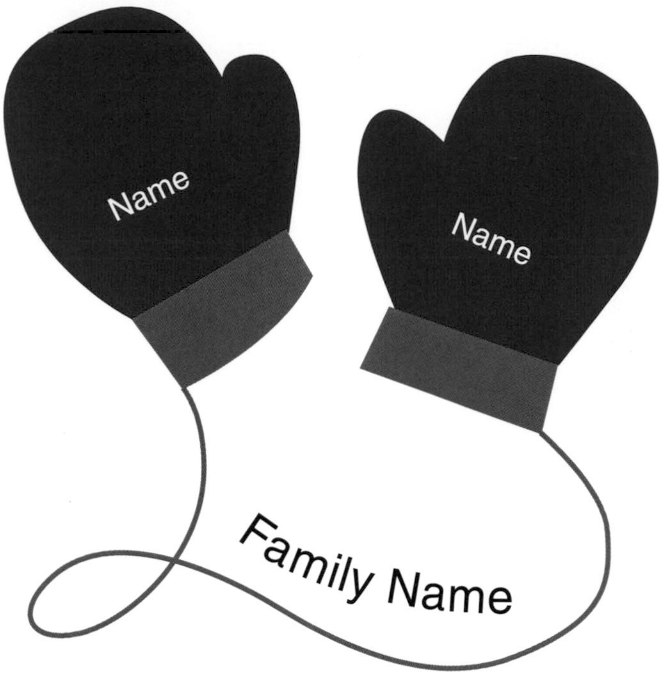
Name
Name
Family Name

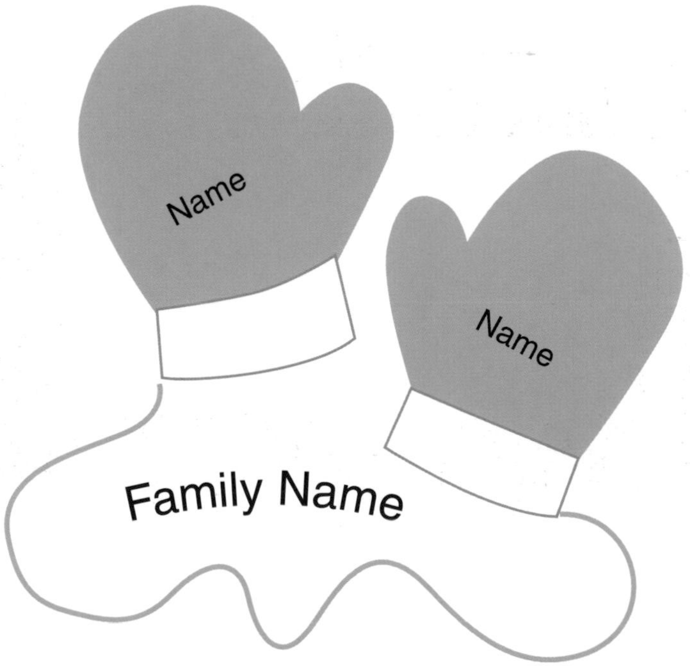
Name
Name
Family Name

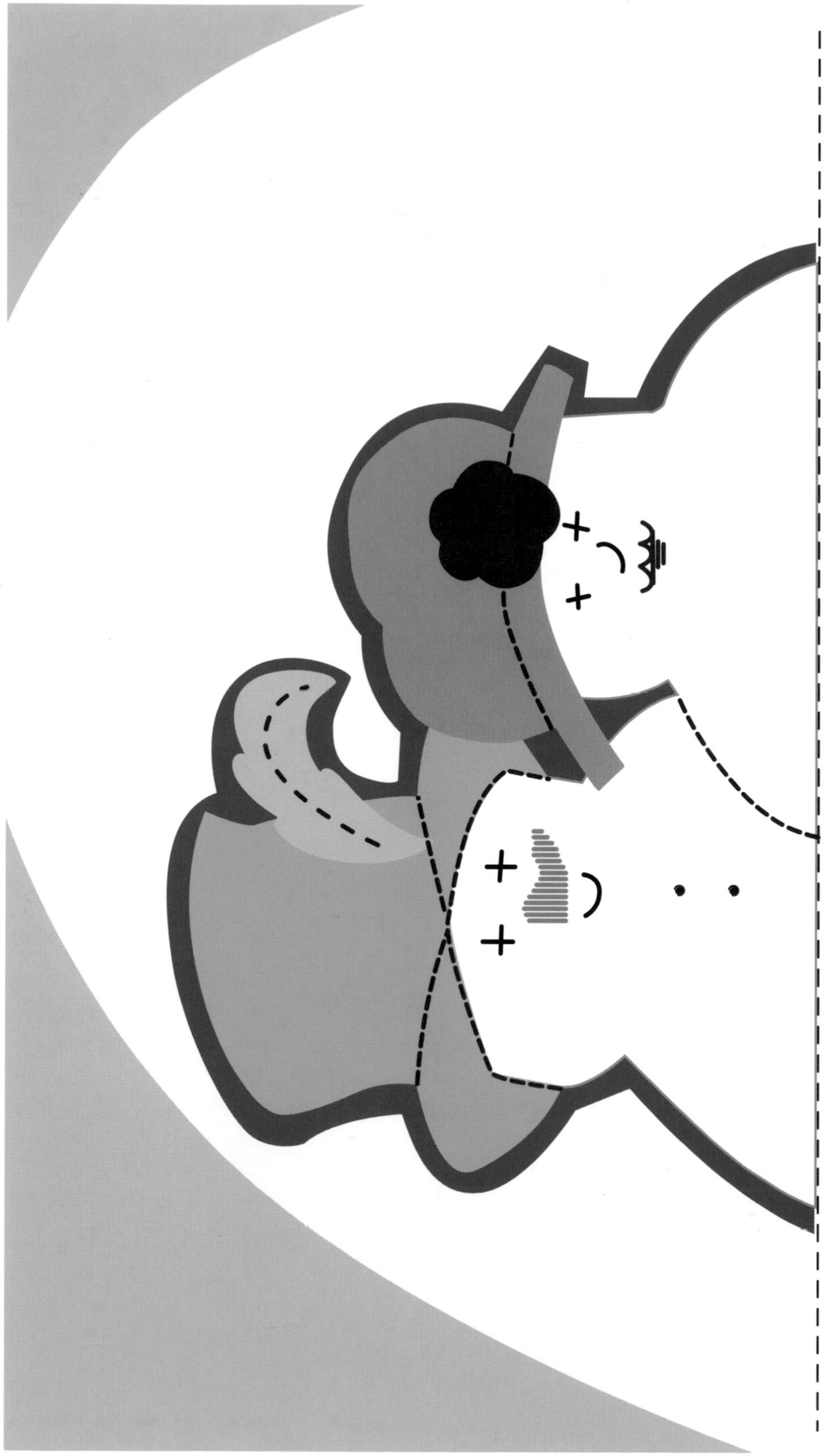

Pattern continues on page 49

Pattern continues on page 48

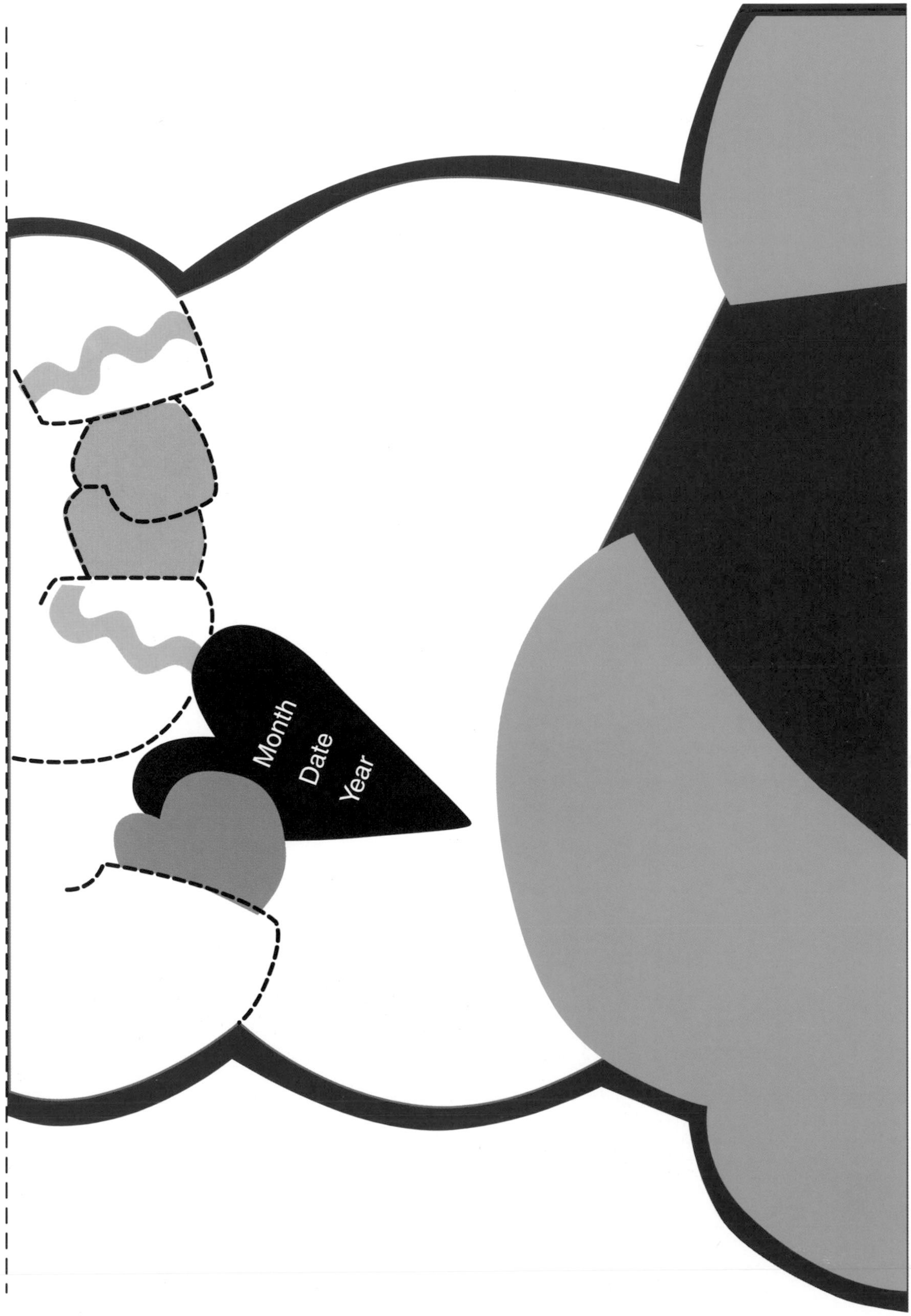

ABCDEFG
HIJKLMN
OPQRSTUV
WXYZ

abcdefghijklmn
opqrstuvwxyz
1234567890

ABCDEFGHI
JKLMNOPQ
RSTUVWXYZ

Circle of Love

Finished size: 14" x 20¾"

Materials

½ yard lavender fabric
½ yard pale lavender fabric
½ yard white felt for backing and small circles
¼ yard blue fabric
2" x 14½" piece of pale pink fabric
Scraps of cotton fabric in these colors: dark olive, olive, pale green, green print, navy blue, royal blue, and blue print
Pale green and blue thread
Embroidery floss in olive, dark brown, lavender, and yellow
Paper-backed fusible web
Blue acrylic paint
Medium-width flat brush
Fine-point permanent markers in white, purple, and black
⅜" dowel, 15" long

Assemble the Background

Refer to "Piecing" on page 7.

1. Cut the following pieces:
   From the lavender, cut:
      3 pieces, each 3⅜" x 7½"
      2 pieces, each 4" x 6½"
      1 piece, 3⅜" x 14½"
   From the pale lavender, cut:
      1 square, 7½" x 7½"
      2 squares, each 4" x 4"
   From the blue, cut:
      1 piece, 7½" x 5⅞"
   From the pale pink, cut:
      1 strip, 2" x 14½"
   From the green print, cut:
      4 strips, each 1⅛" x 7½"
2. Sew each 3⅜" x 7½" lavender piece to a green print strip on the long edge. You will have 3 units, with one green print strip left over.

Make 3

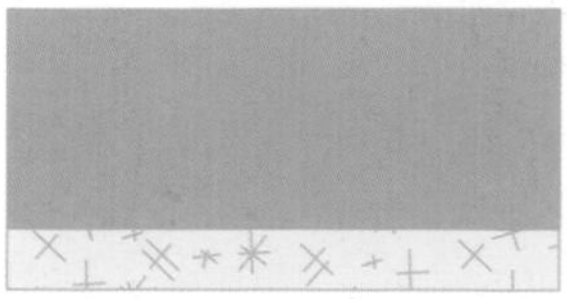

3. Sew a 4" pale lavender square to each short end of 1 unit. Sew the pale pink strip across the top.

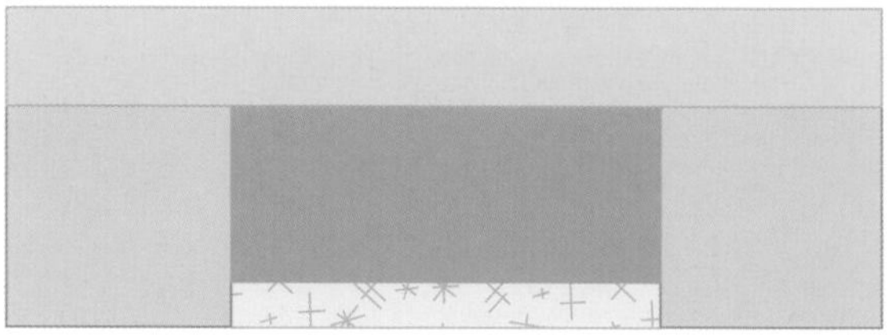

4. Sew the remaining 2 units to opposite sides of the 7½" pale lavender square.

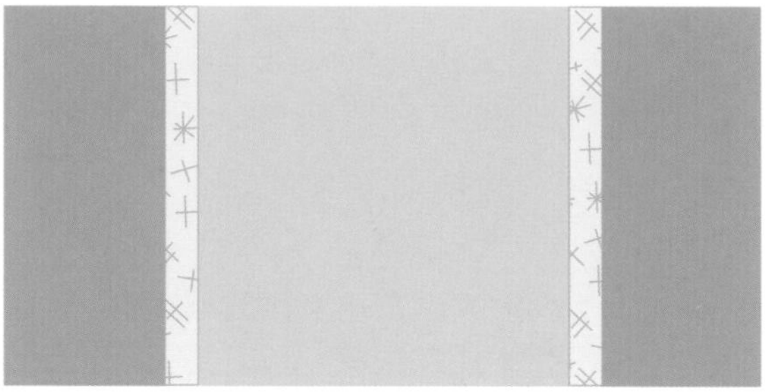

5. Sew the remaining green print strip to one long edge of the 7½" x 5⅞" blue piece.
6. Trace the 2 long blue shapes (page 57) onto tracing paper. Cut out each pattern, pin it to the right side of the blue fabric, and lightly trace its outline. Cut out each fabric shape a scant ¼" outside the outline. Place each shape on a 4" x 6½" lavender piece, right sides up and corners aligned. Appliqué the curved edges only. Sew these appliquéd pieces to each end of the unit made in step 5.

7. Sew the 3 pieced units together. Sew the remaining lavender strip to the bottom.

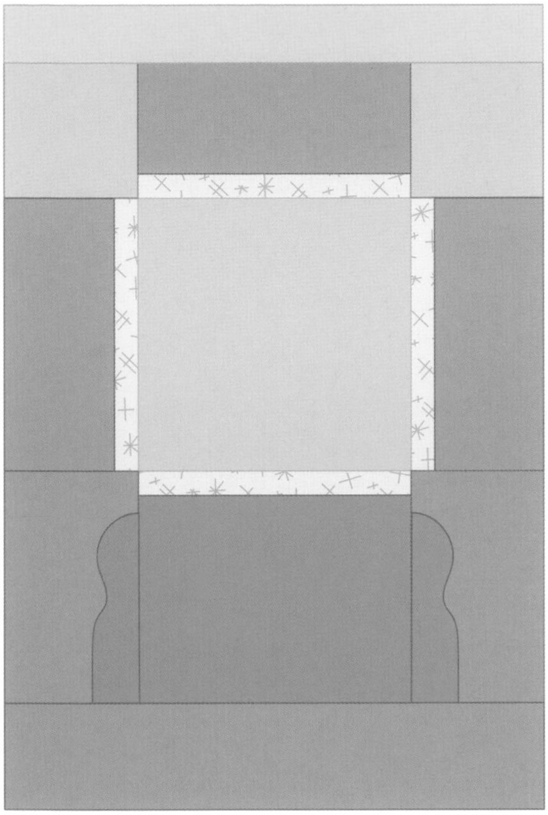

Appliqué the Design

Note: Refer to "Needle-Turn Appliqué" on pages 5–6 and "Fusible Appliqué" on pages 6–7. Refer to the project photo and pattern for placement.

1. Trace the pale green triangle onto tracing paper. Cut out along the lines. Pin the pattern piece to the fabric, mark, and cut out, adding ¼" all around. Use the tracing paper pattern to make a second triangle.
2. Place a triangle in each corner of the pieced unit. Pin in place, then hand appliqué along the diagonal edges. Baste the outside edges in place, stitching a scant ¼" from each edge.

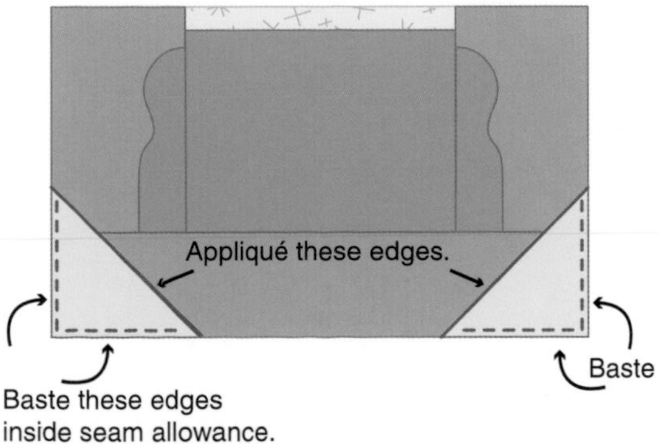

3. Trace the remaining pieces directly from the book onto fusible web (these pieces are symmetrical and don't need to be reversed). For the scallop border pattern, make 1 tracing as is and 2 tracings on the fold so they are twice as long.
4. Cut out each fusible web piece, or group of pieces, leaving a ½" margin all around. Fuse each piece or group to the wrong side of the appropriate fabric.
5. Cut out the 4 dark olive triangles along the marked outlines. Peel off the paper backings. Position each triangle, fusible side down, in a corner of the large pale lavender square. Fuse in place.
6. For each flower, cut out and fuse a dark olive piece, a blue print piece, and a navy blue center. Cut out and fuse the dark olive stems and the lavender shape in the center.
7. Cut out and fuse the 2 blue medallions in the top corners.
8. Cut out and fuse the pale lavender scallop border pieces, trimming the ends to fit against the corner triangles.

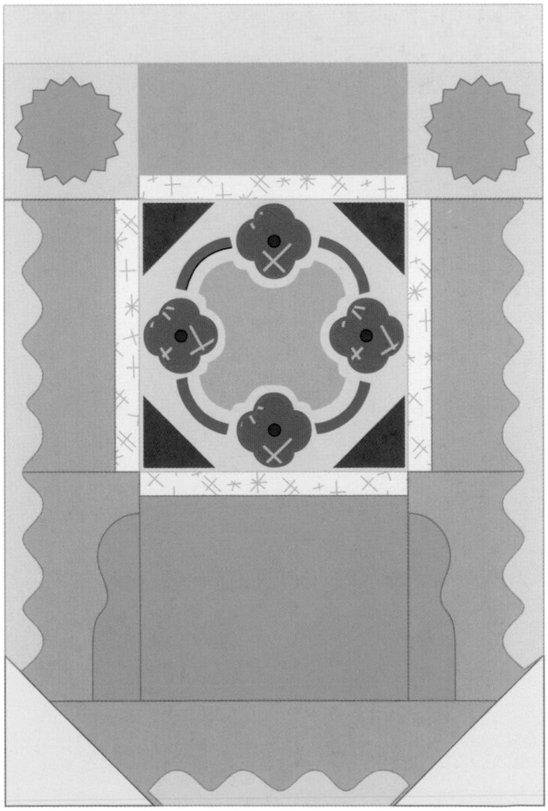

9. Cut out and fuse the small white felt circles, then add a blue swirl piece to each one.

Add the Details

Note: Refer to "Adding the Details" on pages 8–11. Refer to the project photo and pattern for placement.

1. Using an air-soluble or water-soluble pen, draw the flower stems freehand. Using your chosen method, transfer the phrase "Our family is a Circle of Love" and the names in each of the spaces indicated (alphabet appears on page 38).
2. Using 2 strands of olive floss, chain-stitch the heavy flower stems (solid lines). Using 1 strand of olive floss, sew a running stitch for the remaining stems (dashed lines).
3. Using 2 strands of dark brown floss, make long straight stitches in each flower center.
4. Using 2 strands of lavender floss, make long diagonal stitches along the inner edges of the pale green borders, crossing the middle of each stitch with 2 short stitches.
5. Using 2 strands of yellow floss, work a buttonhole stitch along the scalloped edges of the border. Using 1 strand of yellow floss, tack around the edges of each flower and blue medallion as desired.
6. Using the white marker, ink the phrase at the top and the parents' names in the center.
7. Using the purple marker, ink the children's names above the flowers.
8. Using the black marker, ink the grandparents' names in the 2 blue medallions.
9. Using the paint brush and blue paint, add "confetti" to the lavender border areas.

Finish the Wall Hanging

1. From the felt, cut a piece 16" x 24" or slightly larger than the assembled sampler.
2. Layer the felt and the sampler right sides together. Sew around the outside edges of the sampler, leaving a 3" opening for turning. Trim the felt close to the stitching and trim the corners diagonally to eliminate bulk. Turn right side out, and slip-stitch the opening closed. Press.
3. To make a hanging sleeve, cut a 2" x 14" strip of fabric. Fold the short raw edges under twice and hem. Fold the strip in half lengthwise, right sides together, and sew the long edges together with a ¼" seam. Turn the sleeve right side out. Pin the sleeve to the top wrong side of the wall hanging, and slipstitch the top edge. Insert the dowel. Tack the bottom edge of the sleeve to the wall hanging back.

Fabric Key

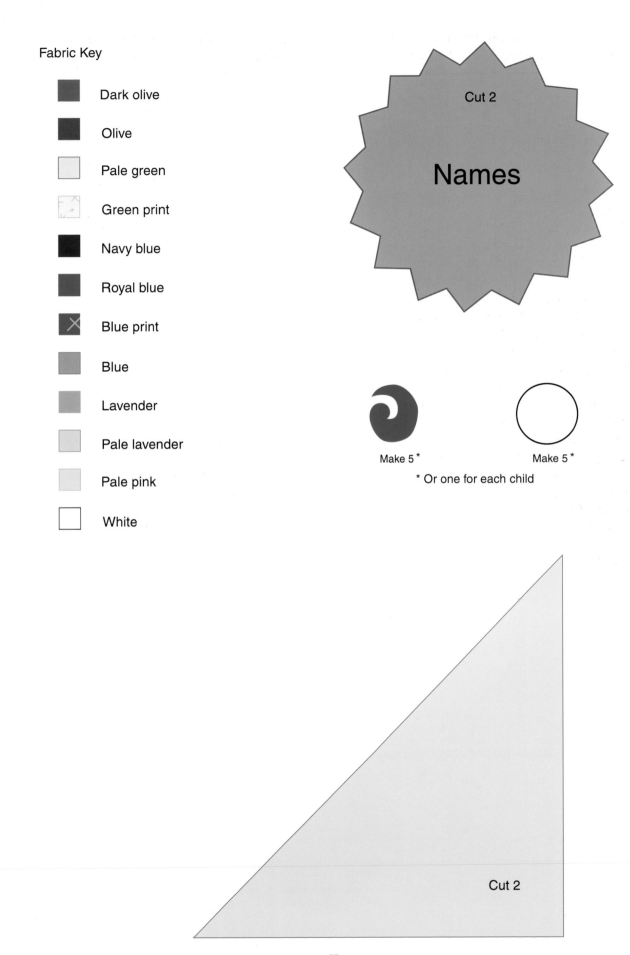

- Dark olive
- Olive
- Pale green
- Green print
- Navy blue
- Royal blue
- Blue print
- Blue
- Lavender
- Pale lavender
- Pale pink
- White

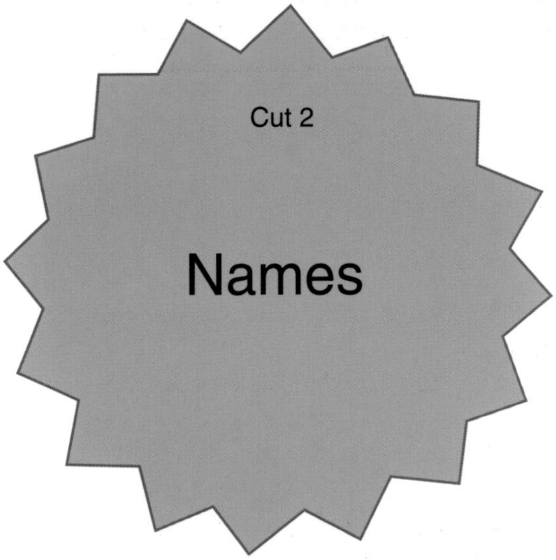

Make 5 *

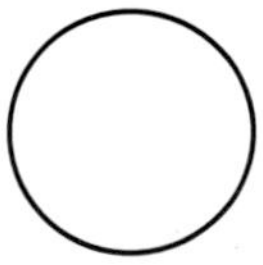

Make 5 *

* Or one for each child

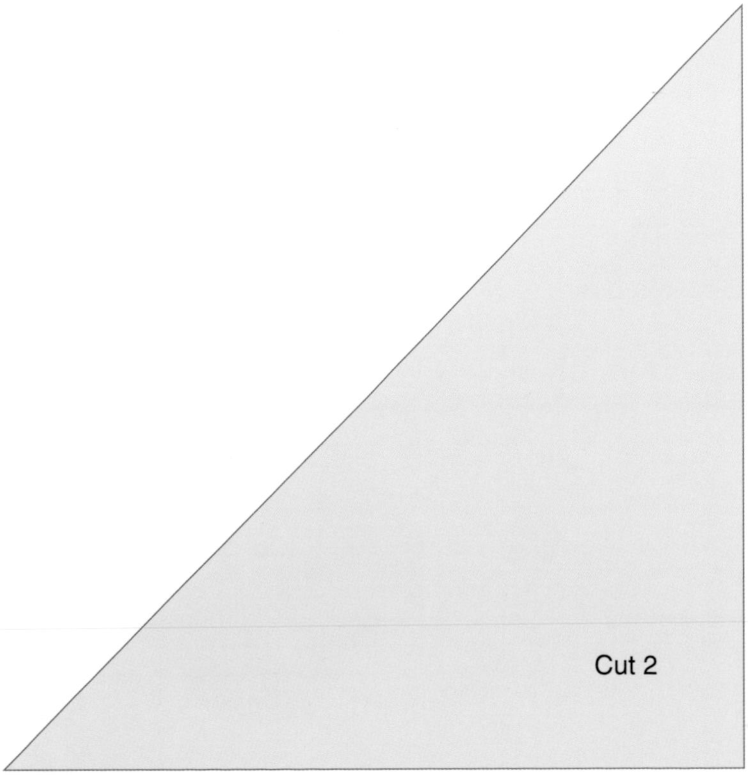

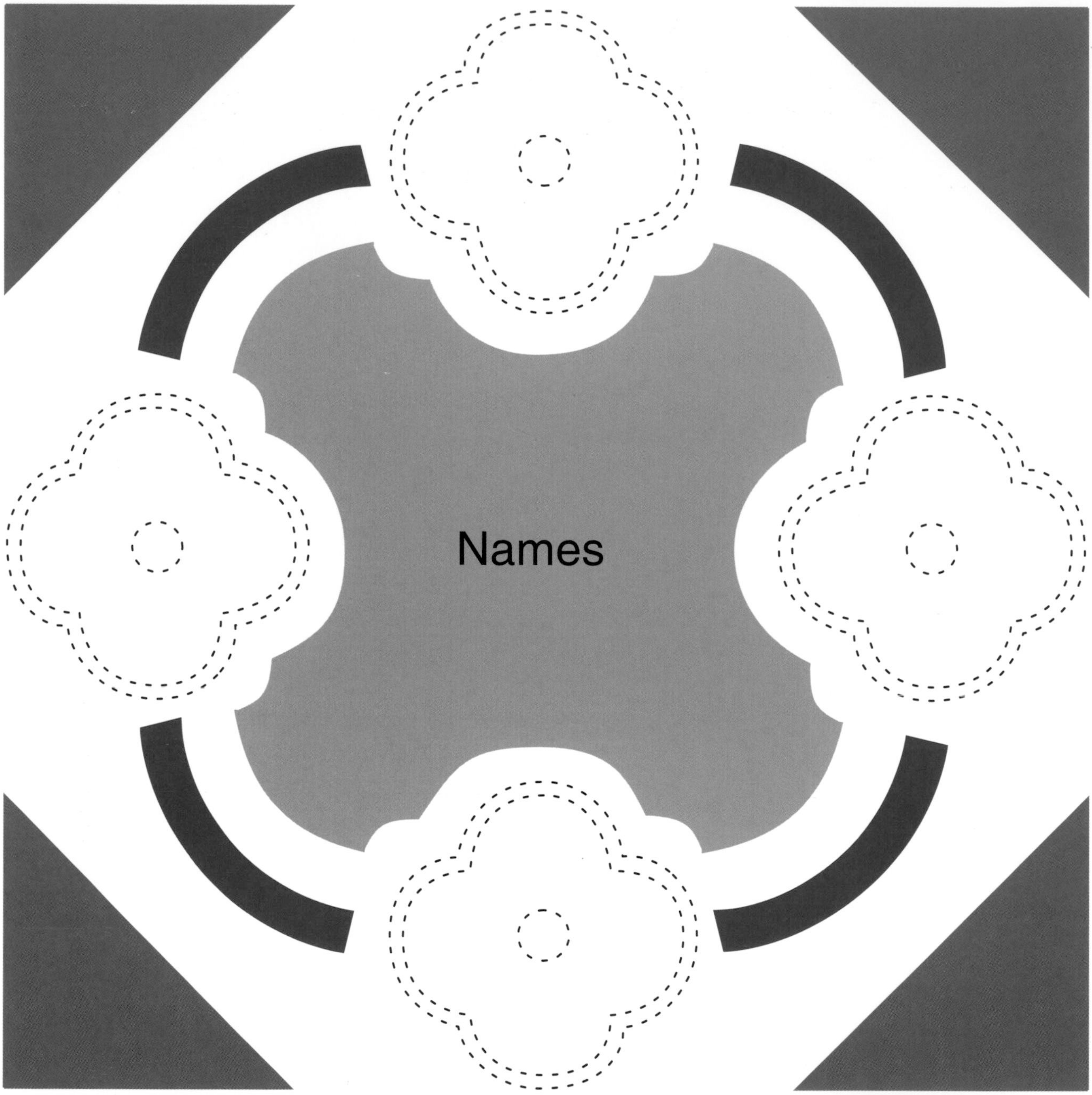
Names

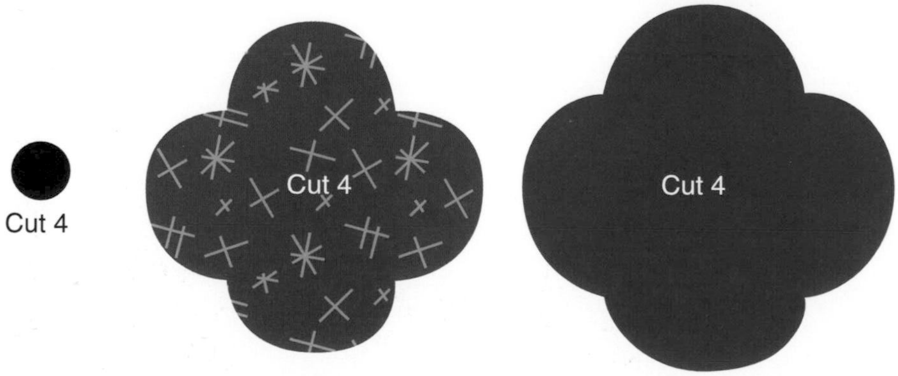
Cut 4
Cut 4
Cut 4

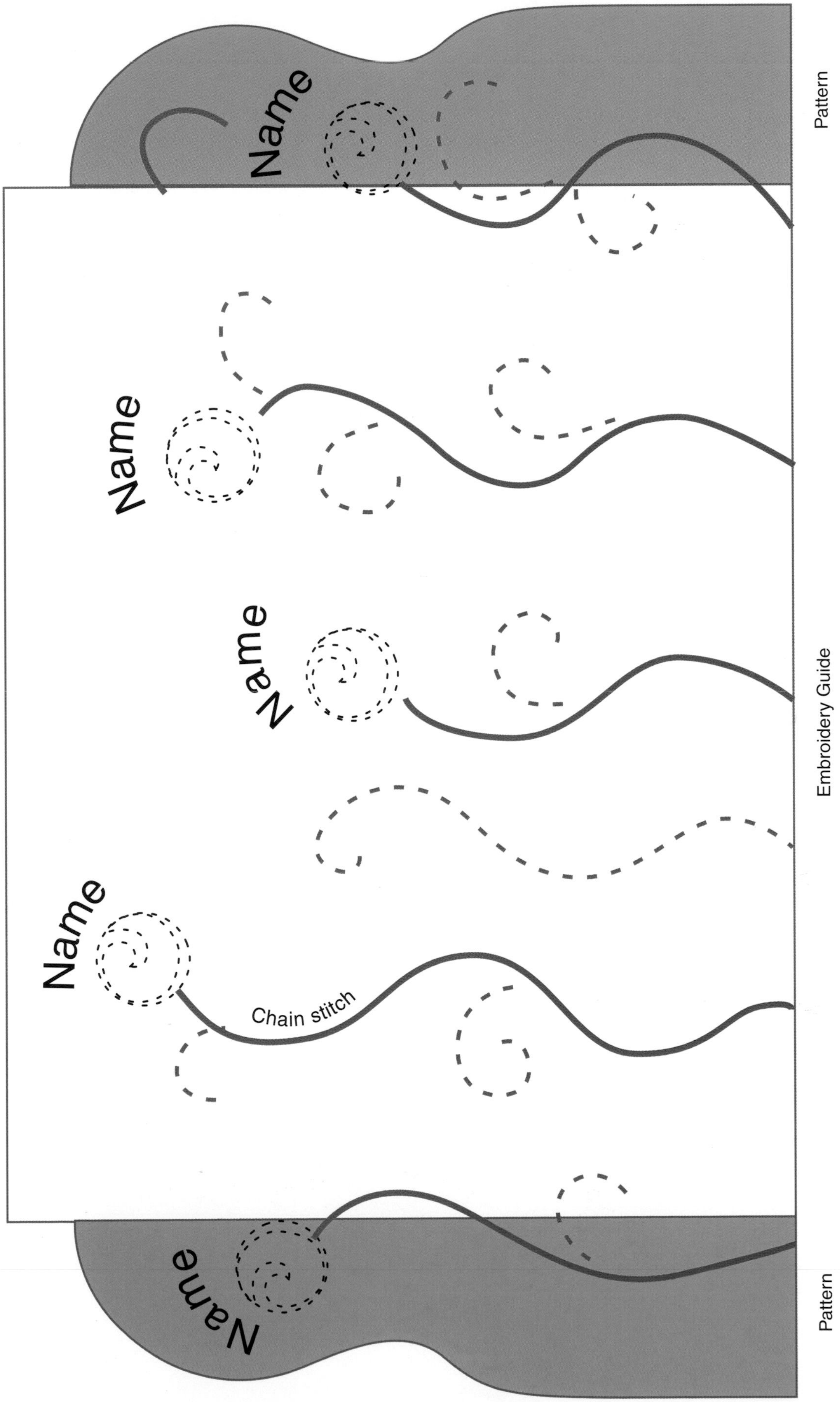
Pattern
Name
Embroidery Guide
Name
Name
Name
Chain stitch
Pattern
Name

Trace 1 as is and 2 on fold.

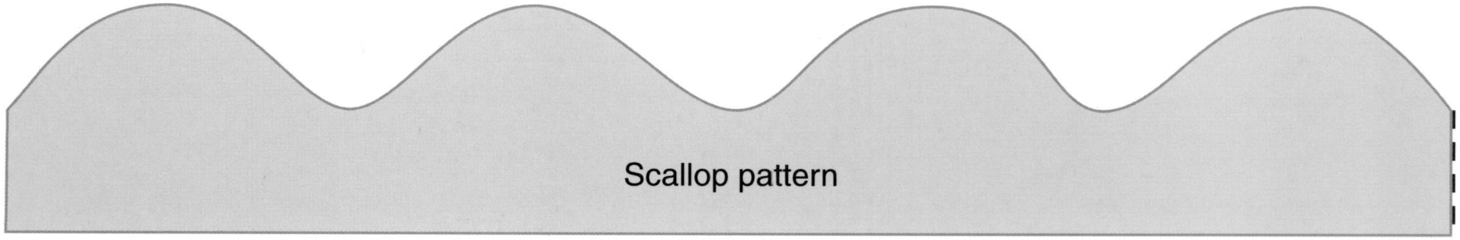
Scallop pattern

Place on fold for 13" strips.

Our family is a
Circle
of Love

Embroidery Guide

Flower Urn

Our Family
Parents
Elliot & Audrey Adams
Children
Matthew James 7·1·2000
John Sinclair 8·8·2000
Children
Suzanne Marie 12·2·2000
Kyle Andrew 11·8·2000
Grandparents
Elliot & Amy Alexander
Grandparents
James & Anna Williams

Finished size: 18" x 29"

Materials

⅜ yard dull green fabric for border
15" x 15" piece of pale pink fabric
10" x 12" piece of cream fabric
7" x 13" piece of gold fabric
6" x 12" piece of green print fabric
Scraps of cotton fabric in these colors: purple, lavender, rose, dusty rose, yellow, dark green, olive, and brown print
Black and gold thread
Embroidery floss in green, dark brown, and light green
Paper-backed fusible web
Fine-point permanent marker in purple

Assemble the Background

1. Cut the following pieces:
   From the pale pink, cut:
      2 pieces, each 4½" x 4"
      1 square, 4" x 4"
      1 piece, 12" x 3¾"
   From the cream, cut:
      2 pieces, each 4½" x 4"
      1 piece, 4" x 12¼"
   From the green print, cut:
      2 pieces, each 4½" x 5¼"
   From the yellow scrap, cut:
      2 pieces, each 4½" x 4"
2. Sew 1 each of the yellow, cream, pale pink, and green print rectangles together along the 4½" edges. Press. Repeat.

Make 2.

3. Sew the 4" x 4" pale pink square to the 4" x 12¼" cream piece. Press.
4. Sew the 3 pieced units together along the long edges, matching seams. Sew the remaining pink strip to the top. Press.

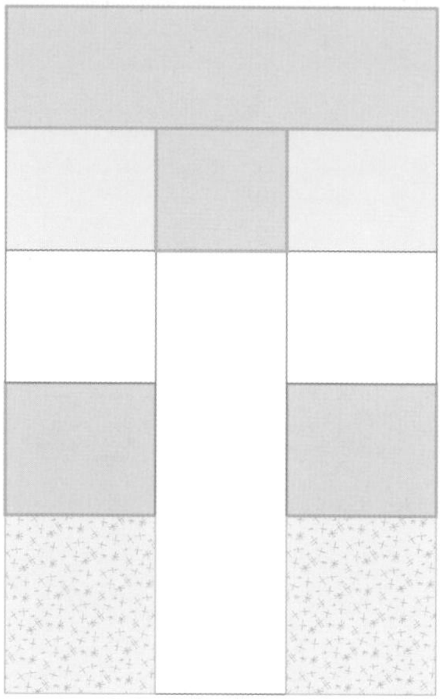

Appliqué the Design

Note: Refer to "Fusible Appliqué" on pages 6–7. Refer to the project photo and pattern for placement.

1. Trace the gold platform pattern onto tracing paper. Cut out along the lines. Fold the gold fabric in half crosswise, right side out, and pin the pattern to it so the dashed line is on the fold.

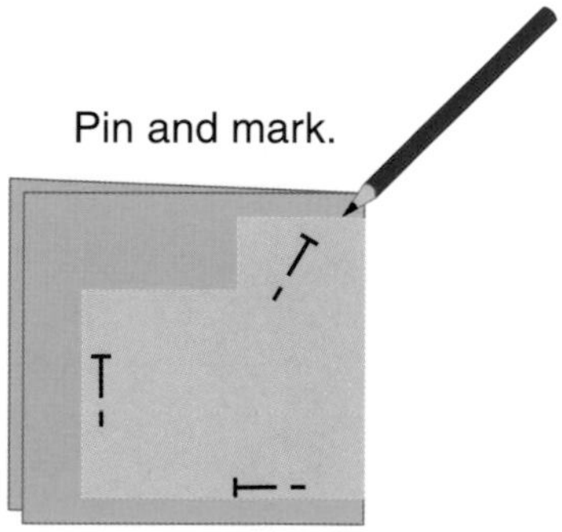

2. Trace along the upper edge of the pattern to mark the appliqué line, then cut out, adding ¼" to all but the folded edge.
3. Unpin and remove the pattern. Then, with the fabric still folded, reposition the pattern on the other side and mark the appliqué fold line as before.

Flip and mark.

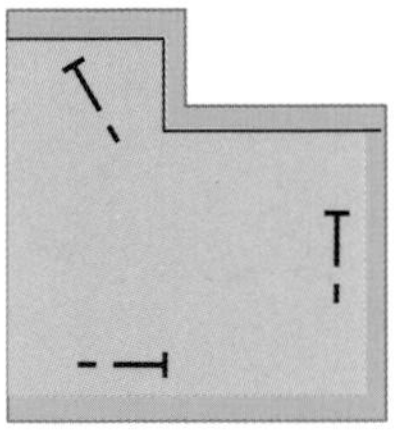

4. Open the gold platform flat. Your fabric should be marked as shown.

Open out.

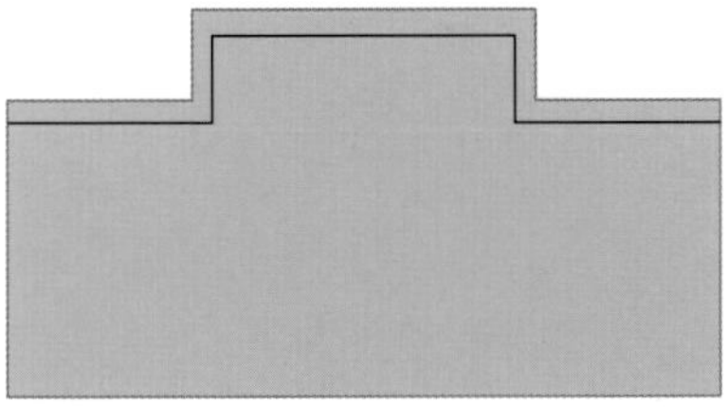

5. Position the gold platform on the pieced panel so it overlaps the lower edge ½" at each side. Pin in place. Turn under and appliqué the overlapping gold edge. On the wrong side, trim the cream and green print fabrics close to the seam allowance.

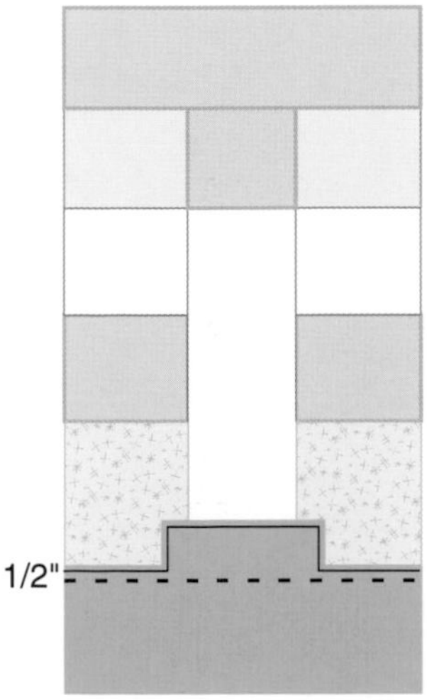

6. Place a 12" x 23" sheet of tracing paper (tape smaller sheets together if necessary) on the pieced fabric background. Using a yardstick and a pencil, lightly trace all seam lines.
7. Using these traced lines as a guide and referring to the diagrams and photo, position the tracing paper on the urn/bouquet pattern on page 64. Trace the urn, pedestal, and all the flowers and stems, including their numbers. In the same way, position the paper to trace the ornament below the pedestal, the 2 flower sprays to either side (trace the stems only—you do not need to trace the flowers), and the 2 small flowers and gold frames near the top.
8. Turn the overlay wrong side up and use it to trace the pattern pieces onto fusible web. Remember to group pieces that will be cut from the same fabric, such as the rose flowers. Copy the numbers onto pieces that have them. Trace the rose and dusty rose flowers for the flower sprays directly from the book until you have the correct number. Cut out each fusible web piece, or group of pieces, leaving a ½" margin all around.
9. Fuse each piece or group to the wrong side of the appropriate fabric.
10. Position the overlay on the pieced background, right sides up. Pin along one edge.
11. Cut out the vase along the marked outline. Peel off the paper backing and position the piece, fusible side down, on the pieced background, using the overlay as a guide. Flip the overlay out of the way and fuse. Cut out and fuse the dusty rose pedestal and the 2 gold frames.
12. Cut out and fuse all the pieces labeled "1."

13. Cut out and fuse all the pieces labeled "2."

14. Cut out and fuse the remaining pieces, including the lavender piece in the dark green frame.

Add the Details

Note: Refer to "Adding the Details" on pages 8–11. Refer to the project photo and pattern for placement.

1. Using an air-soluble or water-soluble pen, draw all embroidered elements freehand. Using your chosen method, transfer the words in script on the pattern and your family names in the designated spaces (alphabet appears on page 38).
2. Using 1 strand of green floss, work "Our Family" at the top of the design in whipped backstitch. Stitch the curved underline with a running stitch.
3. Using 1 strand of dark brown floss, work "Parents," "Children," and "Grandparents" in a whipped backstitch.
4. Using black thread, tack around the edges of the fused pieces as desired. Make star stitches in the centers of 3 flowers and a cross stitch in the center of a fourth.
5. Using 2 strands of light green floss, make French knots in 3 flowers. Sew a running stitch along the upper edge of the platform.
6. Using a purple marker, print the names and birth dates.

Complete the Design

1. From the dull green border fabric, cut 2 strips, each 3½" x 18", and 2 strips, each 3½" x 23"
2. Sew a 23" strip to each side of the assembled piece. Sew the remaining strips to the top and bottom edges.

3. Have the piece professionally framed.

Fabric Key

- Purple
- Lavender
- Rose
- Dusty rose
- Pale pink
- Gold
- Yellow
- Green print
- Dark green
- Olive green
- Brown print

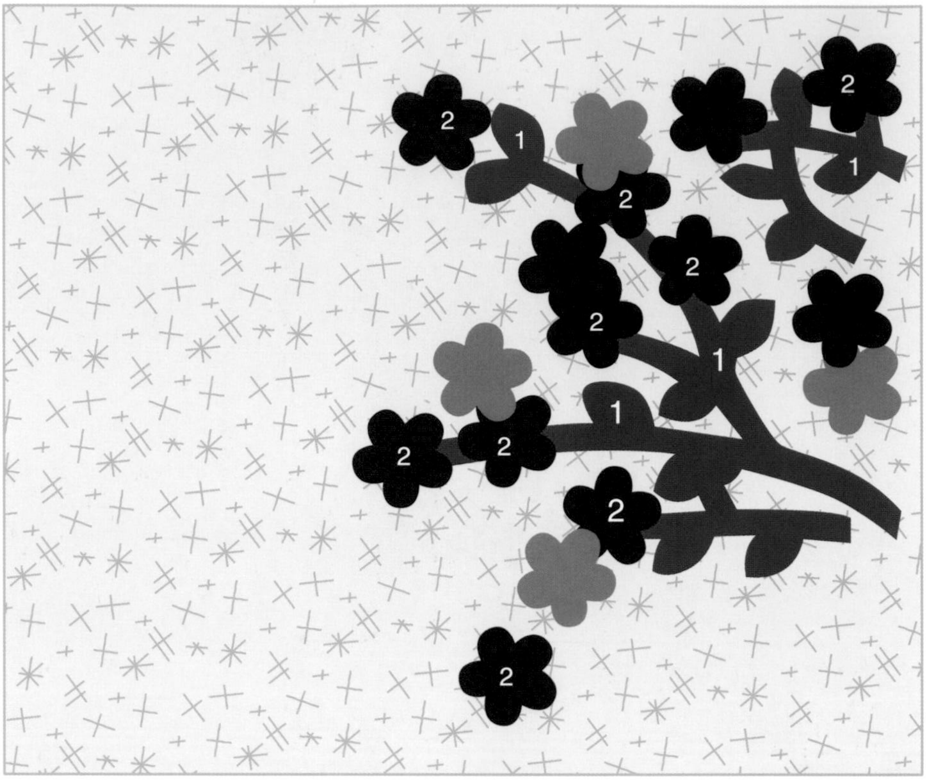

Trace 31.
Fuse 10 to dusty rose.
Fuse 21 to rose.

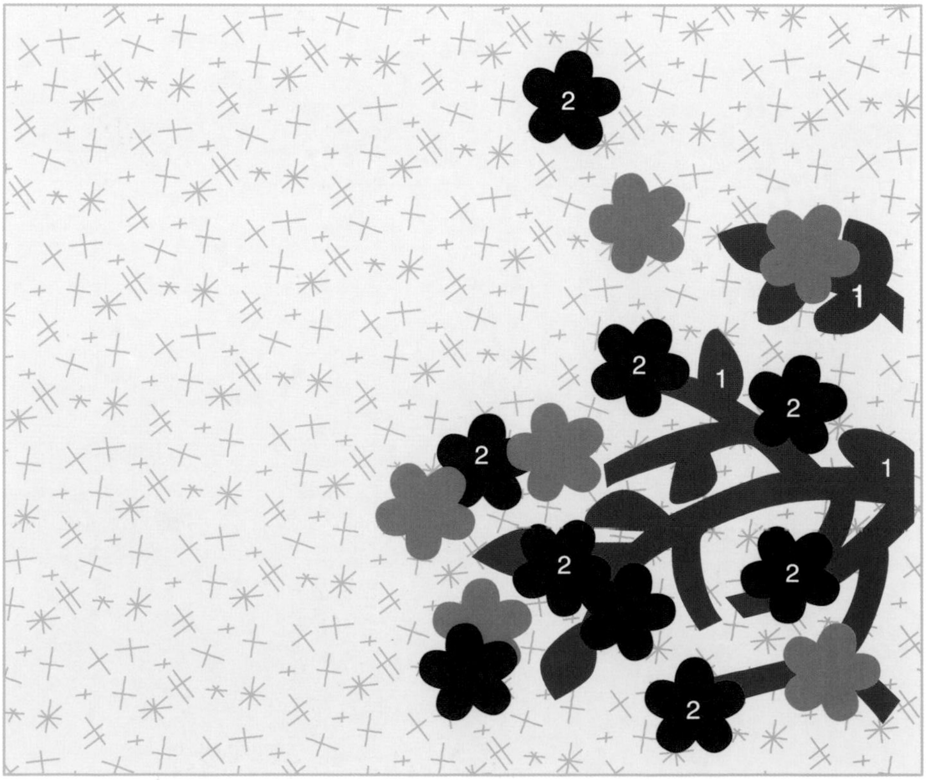

Embroidery Guide

Family Tree Sampler

Finished size: 16" x 22"

Materials

17" x 23" piece of light brown fabric
12" x 12" piece of white fabric
9" x 12" piece of light olive fabric
6" x 12" piece of blue chambray fabric
3" x 14" piece of pale green fabric
Scraps of cotton fabric in these colors: dark green, olive, gray-green, rust, light brown, brown, blue, black print, and navy blue
Thread to match fabrics (except white and blue chambray)
Embroidery floss in tan, dark green, and blue
Dark brown fine- and medium-point permanent markers

Assemble the Background

Refer to "Piecing" on page 7.

1. Cut the following pieces:
   From the white, cut:
   1 piece, 9¾" x 10"
   From the blue chambray, cut:
   1 piece, 4¾" x 10"
   From the pale green, cut:
   1 piece, 2½" x 10"
2. Join these 3 pieces along the 10" edges, with the pale green fabric in the middle. Press toward the darker fabric. Leave the unit on your ironing board, wrong side up. Turn under ¼" on all edges and press.

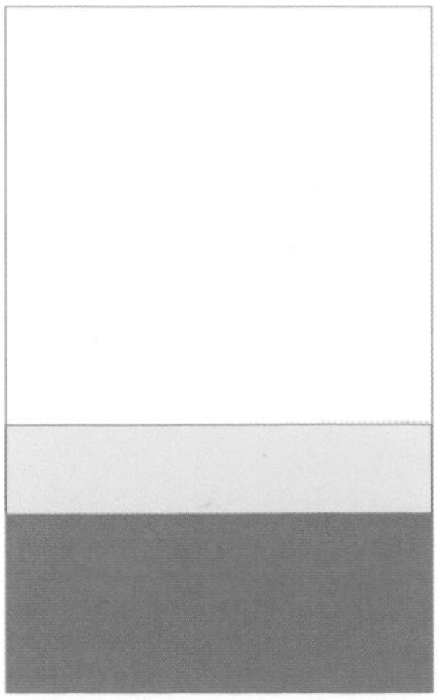

3. If your light brown fabric is larger than 17" x 23", trim it to these exact measurements now. Center the pieced unit on the brown fabric so a 3¾" margin of brown shows all around. Pin in place. Hand-appliqué.

Appliqué the Design

Note: Refer to "Needle-Turn Appliqué" on pages 5–6. Refer to the project photo and pattern for placement.

1. Trace the patterns individually onto tracing paper. Note that the banner is cut out and appliqued in 5 sections. Be sure to transfer the numbers onto these and the 2 acorn patterns. Cut out along the lines. Pin each pattern piece to right side of the desired fabric, mark, and cut out, adding a scant ¼" all around.
2. Appliqué the navy blue zigzag strip to the bottom edge of the blue chambray section.

3. Position the dark green leaf section on the left side of the white background. Appliqué the left and lower edges only.

4. Appliqué the olive piece, stitching down all but the 4" section that will be covered by the trunk.
5. Pin the tree trunk to the background. Pin the small gray-green piece so it overlaps the higher branch but tucks under the lower branch. Appliqué the gray-green piece, then the trunk.

6. Appliqué the 4 remaining leaf pieces.
7. To position the banner, start with piece #5. Pin it in place on the background. Next, tuck pieces #3 and #4 under the lower edge with ½" of overlap, referring to the pattern for placement. The marked appliqué lines should line up (stick a pin through from the top to check). Pin in place. Now tuck pieces #1 and #2 under the ends of the banner, again overlapping by ½". Pin. Appliqué in numerical order, skipping any edge that is covered by another piece.
8. Appliqué the 2 heart shapes, then the 3 acorns.

Add the Details

Note: Refer to "Adding the Details" on pages 8–11. Refer to the project photo and pattern for placement.

1. Using your chosen method, transfer your family names and dates in each of the spaces indicated (alphabets appear on page 76).
2. Using 2 strands of tan floss, sew a running stitch around the tree trunk.
3. Using 1 strand of dark green floss, work a buttonhole stitch along the top edge of the chambray piece.
4. Using 1 strand of blue floss, satin-stitch the lines on the 3 acorns.
5. Using the dark brown markers, print the names and dates in the spaces indicated. Make small, straight lines for the acorn stems.
6. Have the piece professionally framed.

Fabric Key

- Dark green
- Olive green
- Light Olive
- Gray green
- Pale green
- Rust
- Brown
- Light brown
- Blue
- Chambray
- Black print
- Navy blue
- White

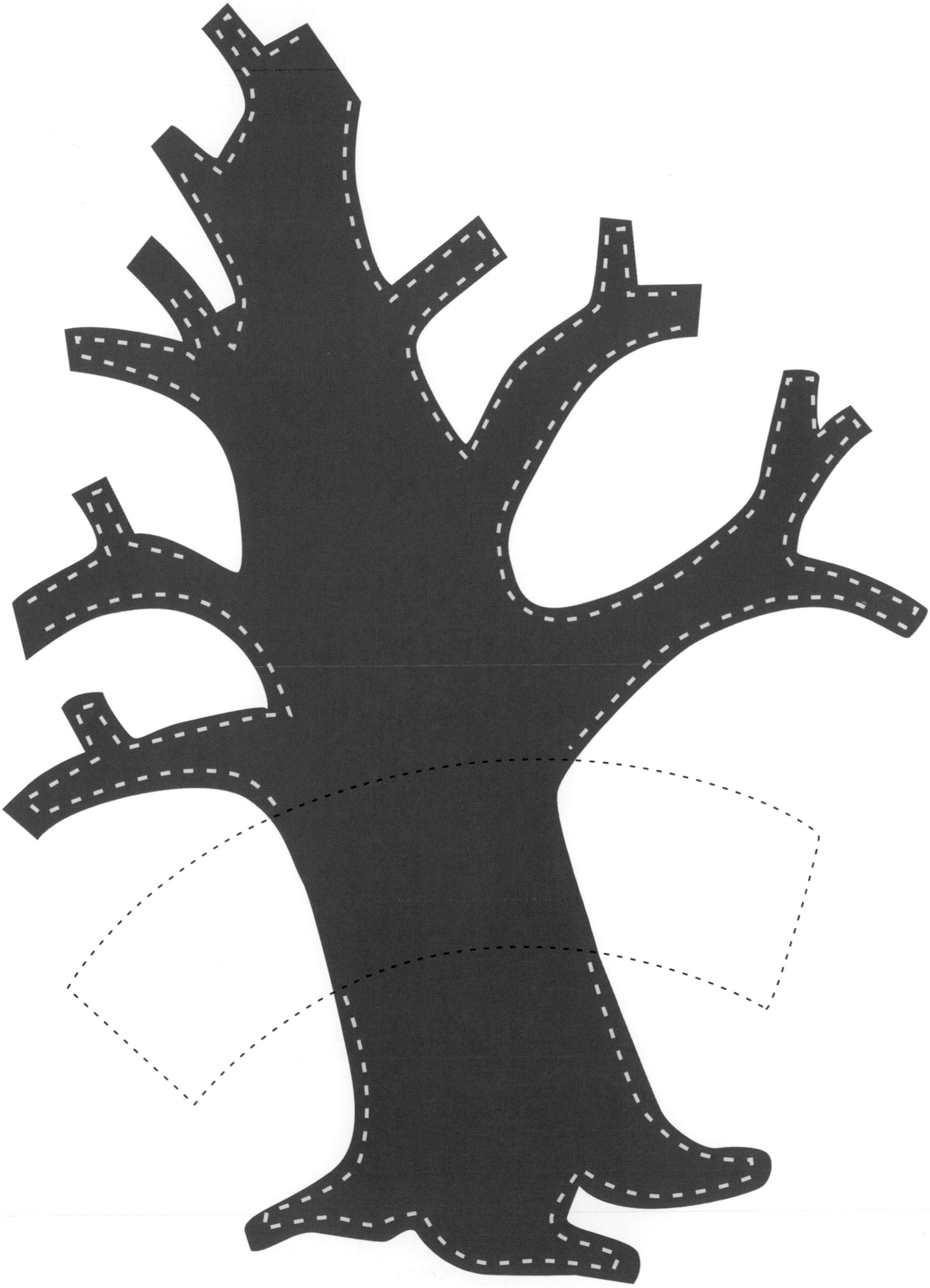

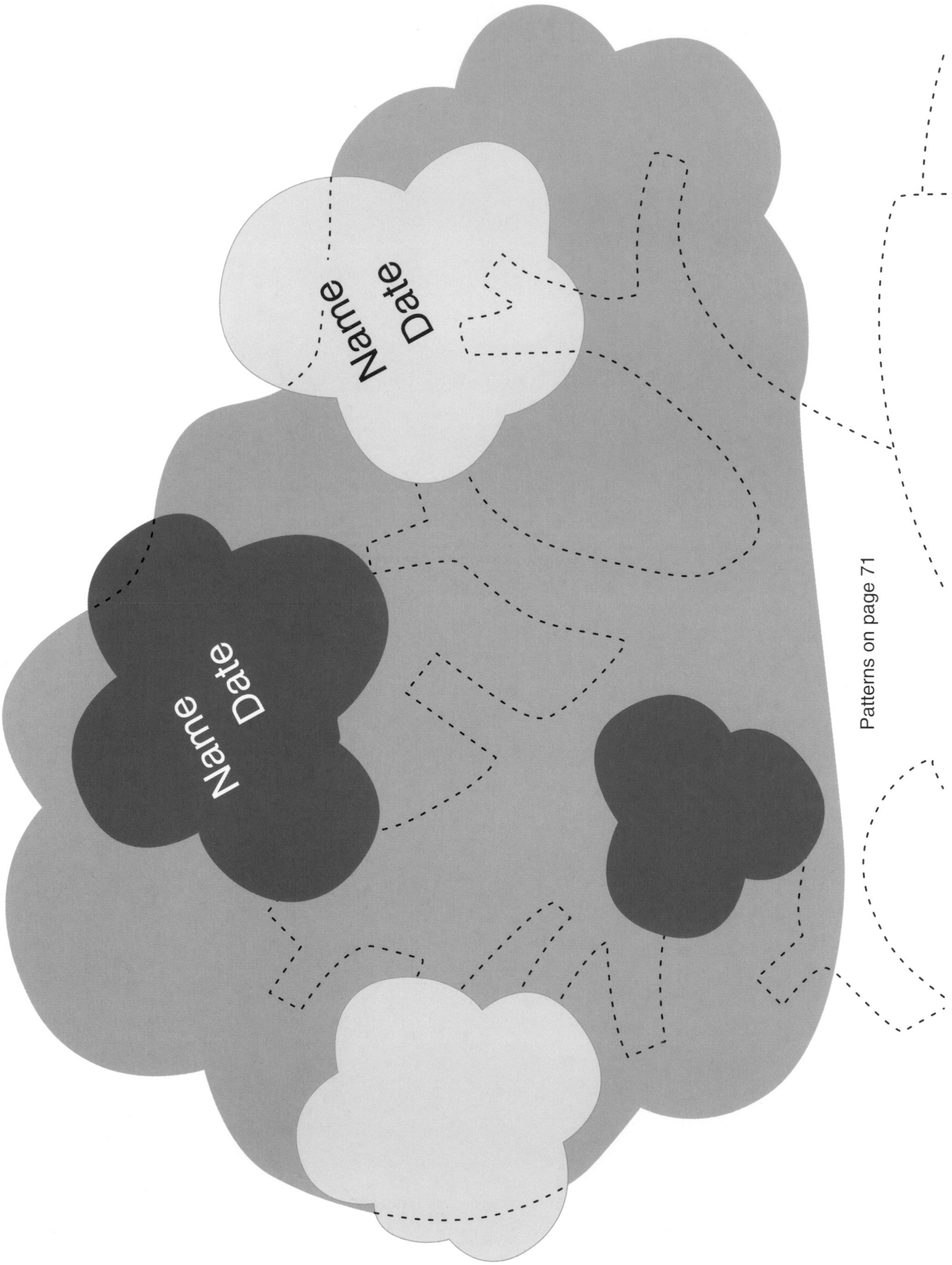
Name
Date
Name
Date
Patterns on page 71

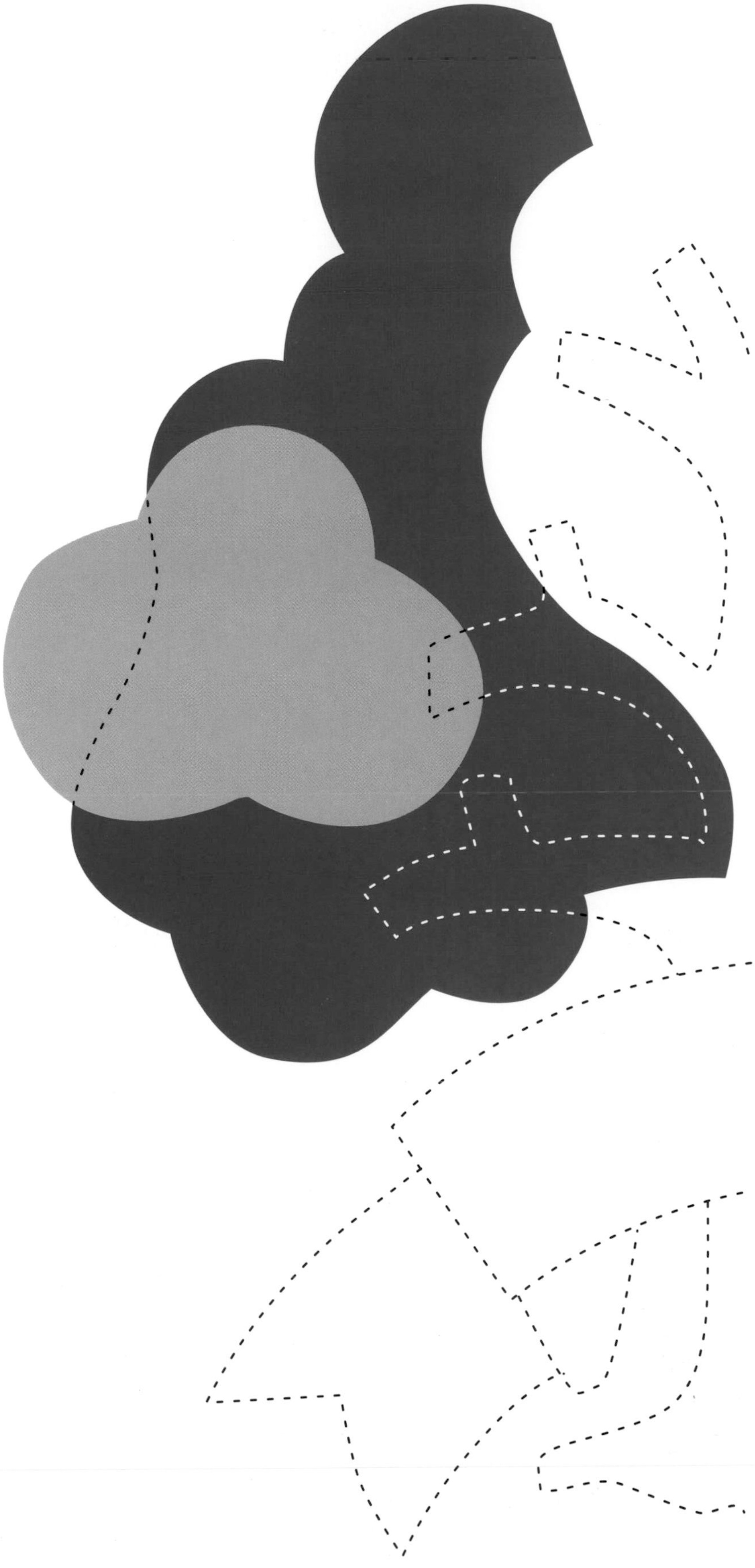

Family Name
5
2
4
3
1
Trace and cut out in 5 sections.
Appliqué in numerical order.

Cut 3 of each piece.

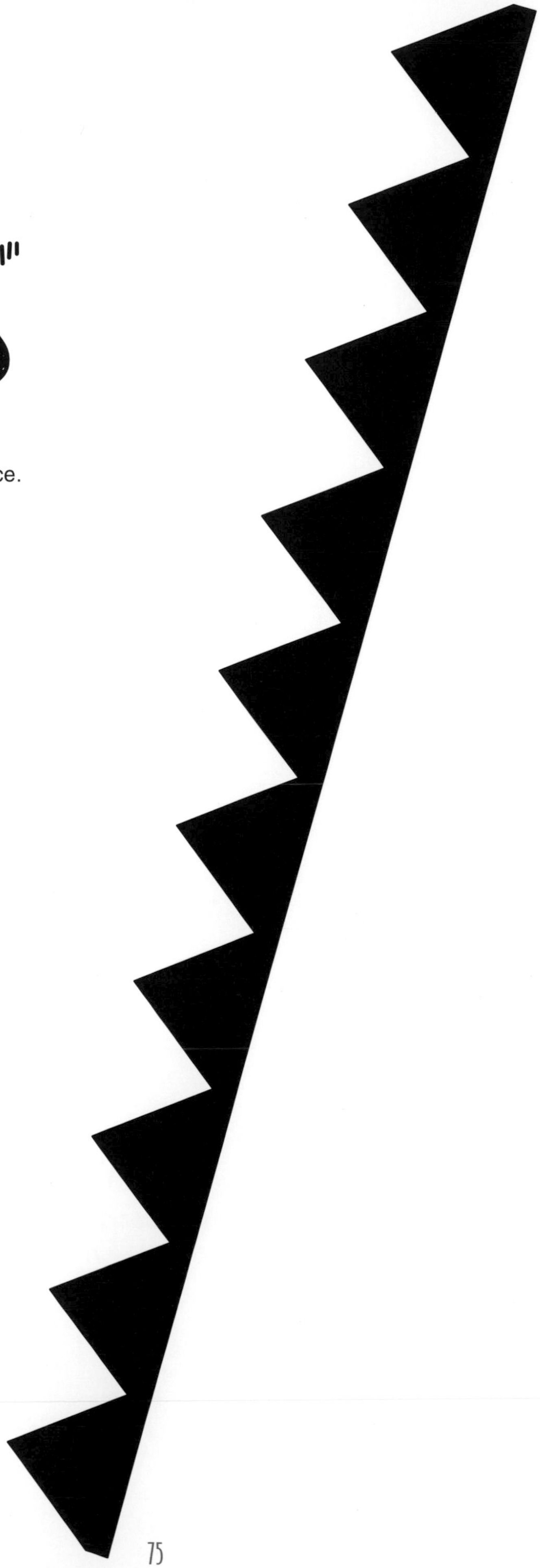

ABCDEFG
HIJKLMN
OPQRSTUV
WXYZ

abcdefghijk
lmnopqrst
uvwxyz

ABCDEFGHIJKLMN
OPQRSTUVWXYZ
abcdefghijklmno
pqrstuvwxyz
1234567890

Boat Sampler

Finished size: Art is 15½" x 20";
12½" x 18" shows within the frame

Materials

¼ yard green fabric
12" square of royal blue fabric
5" x 15" piece of navy blue fabric
Scraps of cotton fabric in these colors: dark red, rose, pink print, gold print, gold, yellow, cream, brown, bright blue, blue-gray, and black print
Thread to match fabrics (except royal, rose, dark red, and gold print)
Embroidery floss in dark green, blue-gray, tan, white, gold, and dark gold
Paper-backed fusible web
Fine-point permanent markers in tan and black

Assemble the Background

Refer to "Piecing" on page 7 and "Mitering Corners" on page 7.

1. Cut the following pieces:
   From the green, cut:
   - 2 strips, each 3" x 13½"
   - 1 strip, 3" x 16"
   - 1 strip, 10½" x 5"

   From the dark red scrap, cut:
   - 2 rectangles, each 3" x 5"

   From the rose scrap, cut:
   - 2 strips, each ⅝" x 10¾"
   - 1 strip, ⅝" x 10½"
2. Trim your royal blue fabric to 10¼" x 10¾". With right sides together, sew a 10¾" rose strip to each side of the royal blue piece. Sew the remaining rose strip to the top of the royal blue piece. Press toward the rose.
3. Place a 13½" green strip on each side of the background, right sides together and lower edges even. Stitch the pieces together, starting at the lower edge and stopping ¼" from the upper edge of the rose border. Press the seam allowances toward the border.

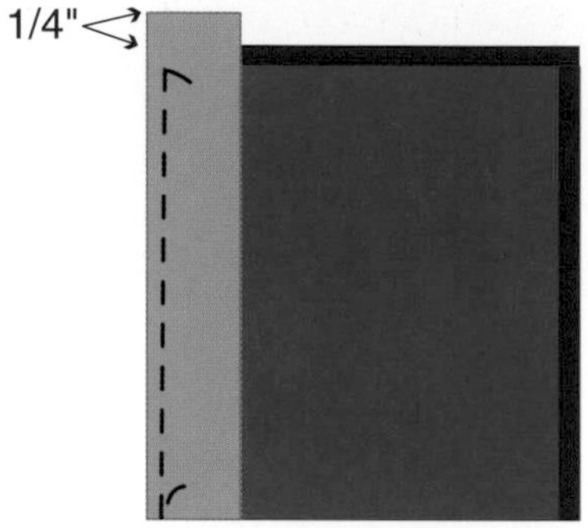

4. Pin to mark the midpoint of the 16" green strip and the midpoint of the top edge of the background.

Pin to mark centers.

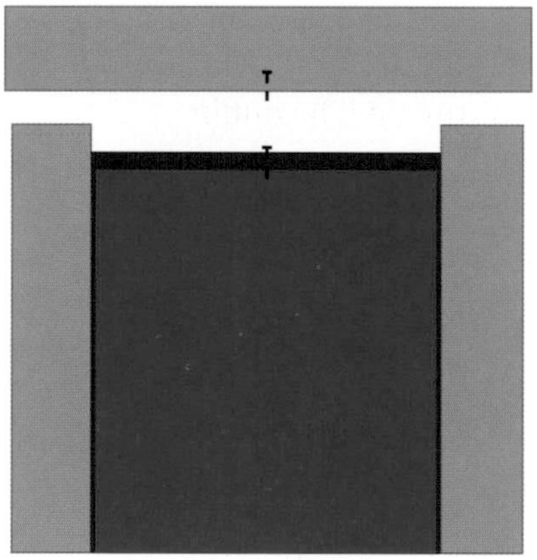

5. Place the strip on the background, right sides together and midpoints matching. Stitch the pieces together, starting and stopping at the side green border seams. Press toward the border.

Stitch, starting and stopping at previous rose/green seams.

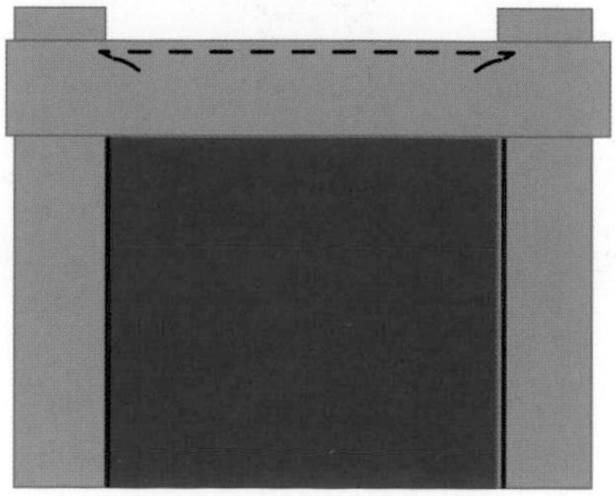

6. Miter the corners. Trim and press.

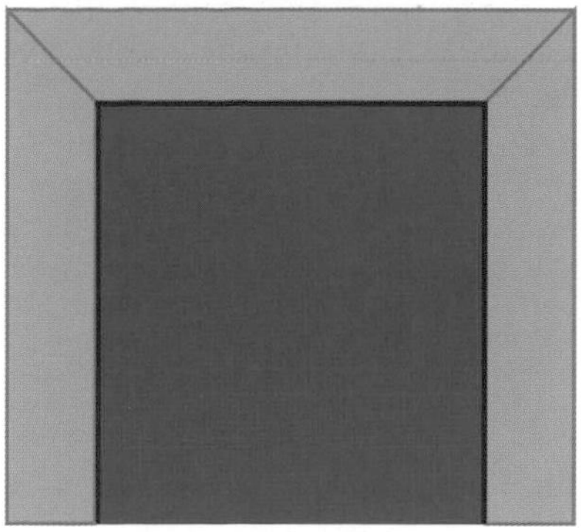

Appliqué the Design

Note: Refer to "Needle-Turn Appliqué" on pages 5–6 and "Fusible Appliqué" on pages 6–7. Refer to the project photo and pattern for placement.

1. Trace all the patterns except the heart, anchors, clouds, and zigzag strip individually onto tracing paper. Cut out each pattern, pin it to the right side of the desired fabric, and lightly trace its outline. Cut out each fabric shape a scant ¼" outside the outline.
2. Appliqué the cream sails, then the top and side edges of the pink boat. Position the upper blue-gray wave on the background so that it overlaps the bottom of the pink boat by about ½" and the left edge is flush with the background. Appliqué the top of the wave. Appliqué the brown sails and the top and sides of the black print boat.

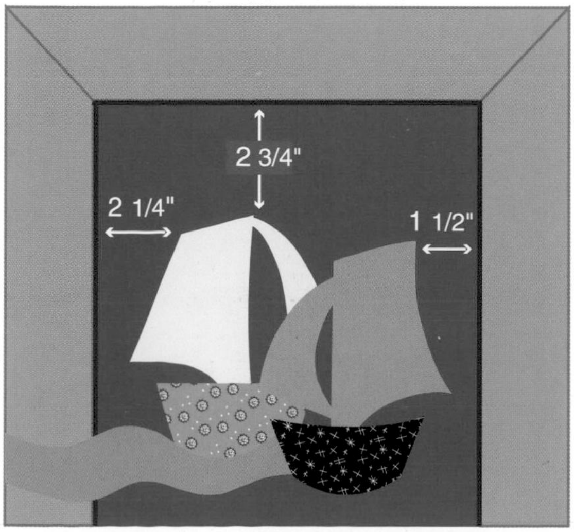

3. Appliqué the yellow banner. Appliqué the top edge of the navy blue wave, then the top edge of the remaining blue-gray wave.

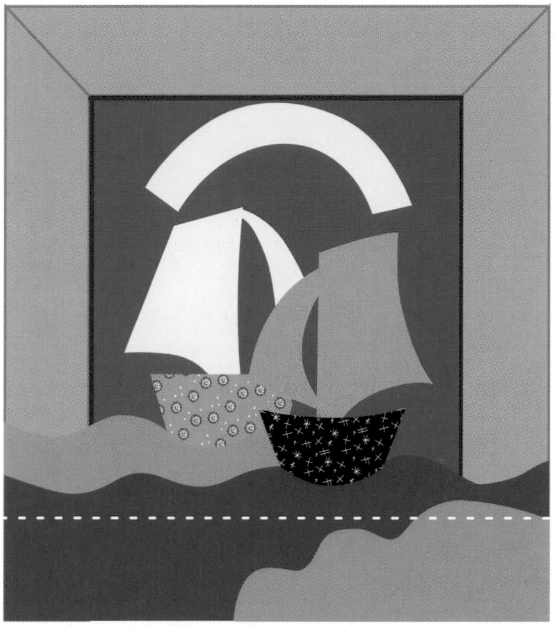

4. Sew a 3" x 5" dark red rectangle to each end of the remaining green strip.

5. Sew the green/red pieced strip to the bottom of the background. Beginning with the yellow fish on the left, appliqué the fins, the body, and the face. Repeat to appliqué the other 2 fish.
6. Trace each cloud onto tracing paper. Turn the tracing paper wrong side up, and use it to trace the clouds onto fusible web. Trace the remaining pieces directly from the book onto the fusible web (these pieces are symmetrical and don't need to be reversed).
7. Cut out each fusible web piece, leaving a ½" margin all around. Fuse each piece to the wrong side of the appropriate fabric.

8. Cut out 1 cloud along the marked outline. Peel off the paper backing, and position the piece, fusible side down, on the background at one corner. Fuse in place. Cut and fuse the remaining cloud. Cut and fuse the anchors, the heart, and the zigzag strip.

Add the Details

Note: Refer to "Adding the Details" on pages 8–11. Refer to the project photo and pattern for placement.

1. Using an air-soluble or water-soluble pen, draw the squiggles at the ends of the banner, the masts, and the wave lines freehand. Using your chosen method, transfer the words "the" and "Married" and all the names and dates in the spaces indicated.
2. Using 1 strand of dark green floss, backstitch the family name on the yellow banner.
3. Using 1 strand of tan floss, sew a running stitch for the squiggles at the ends of the banner.
4. Using 2 strands of blue-gray floss, sew a running stitch for the wave lines. Tack along the upper edge of the blue-gray zigzag piece.
5. Using 1 strand of white floss, sew a running stitch around the clouds. Also backstitch the word "Married" and the date at the bottom of the design. Make French knots for the dots next to the word "Married."
6. Using 1 strand of gold floss, work a buttonhole stitch around each anchor.
7. Using 1 strand of dark gold floss, satin-stitch the 2 masts.
8. Using the black and tan markers, ink the parents' and children's names.
9. Have the piece professionally framed. The frame shown is 16¾" x 22" and has a 2"-wide beveled mat.

Fabric Key

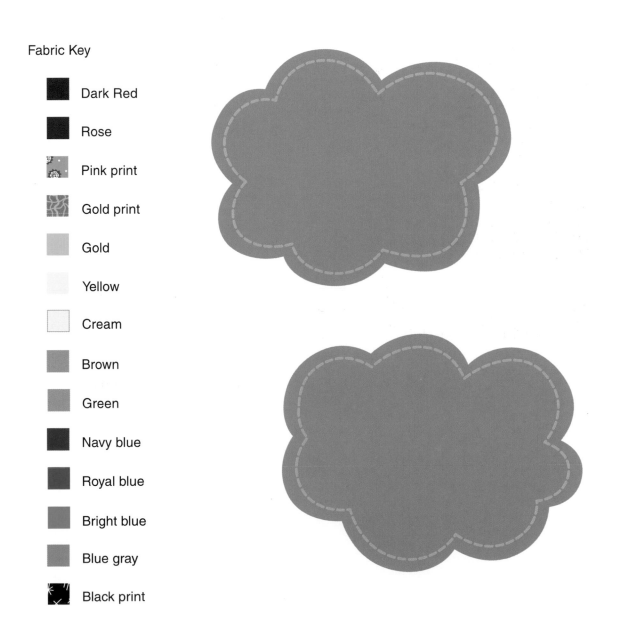

- Dark Red
- Rose
- Pink print
- Gold print
- Gold
- Yellow
- Cream
- Brown
- Green
- Navy blue
- Royal blue
- Bright blue
- Blue gray
- Black print

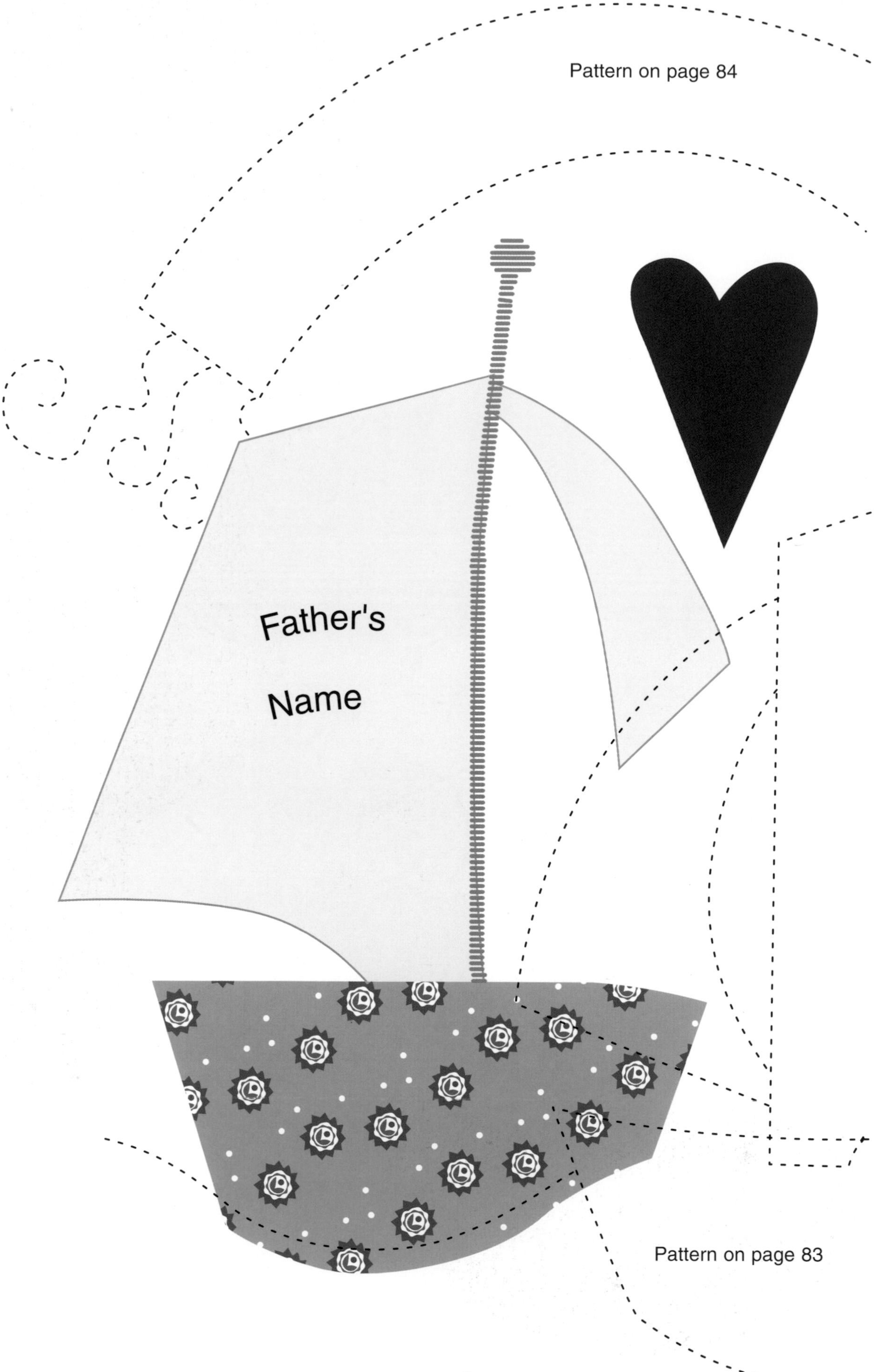
Pattern on page 84
Father's
Name
Pattern on page 83

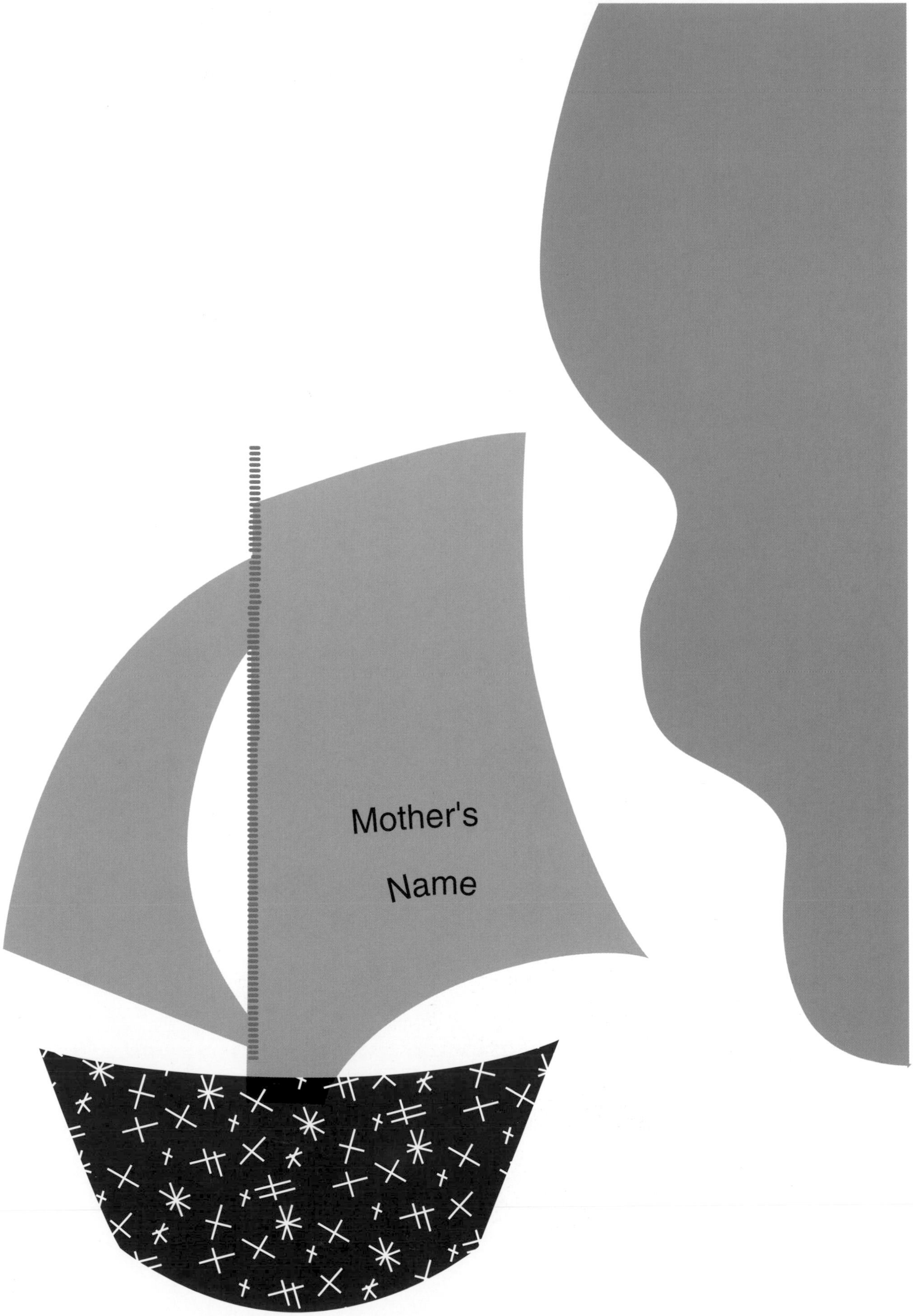
Mother's
Name

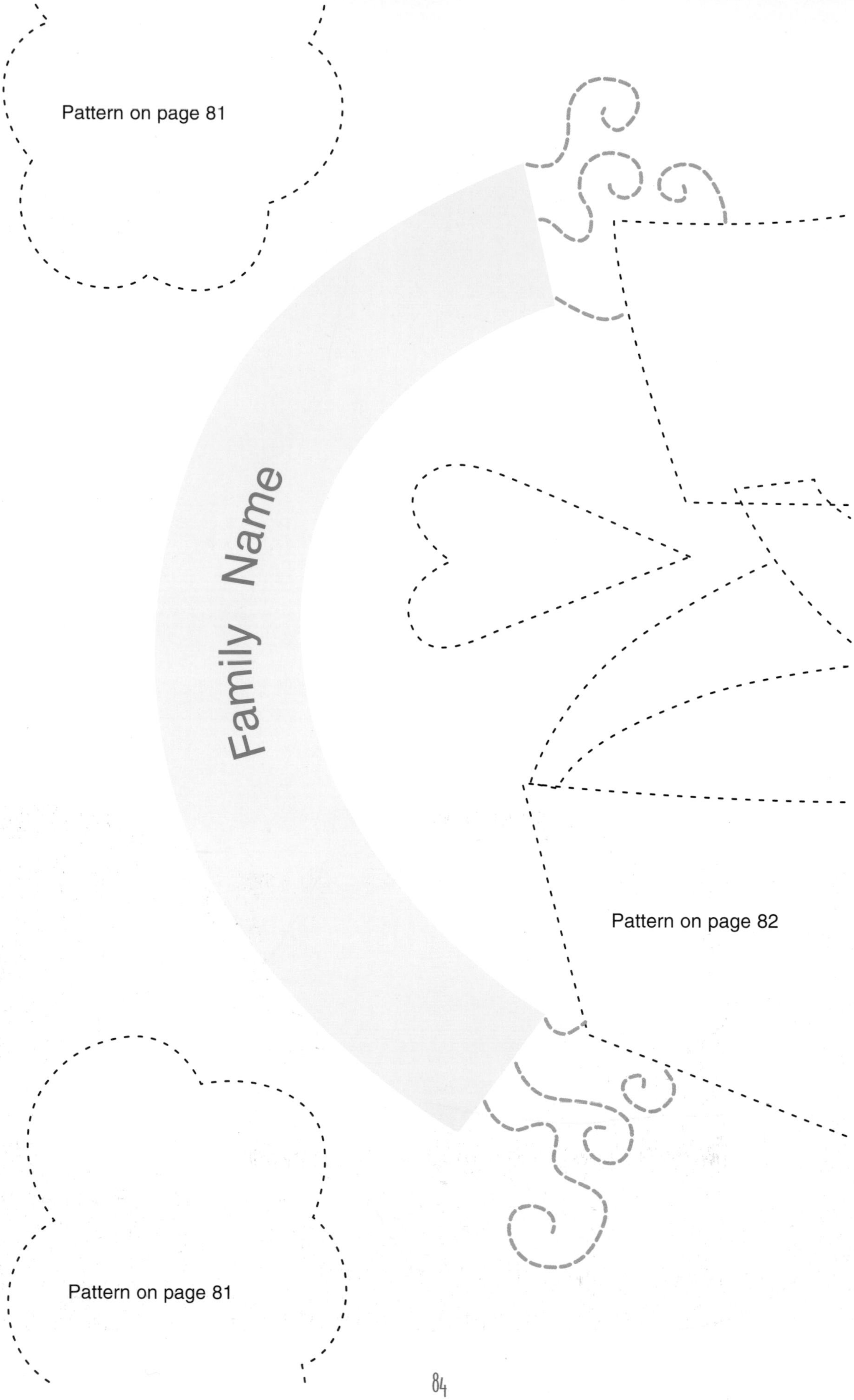
Pattern on page 81
Family Name
Pattern on page 82
Pattern on page 81

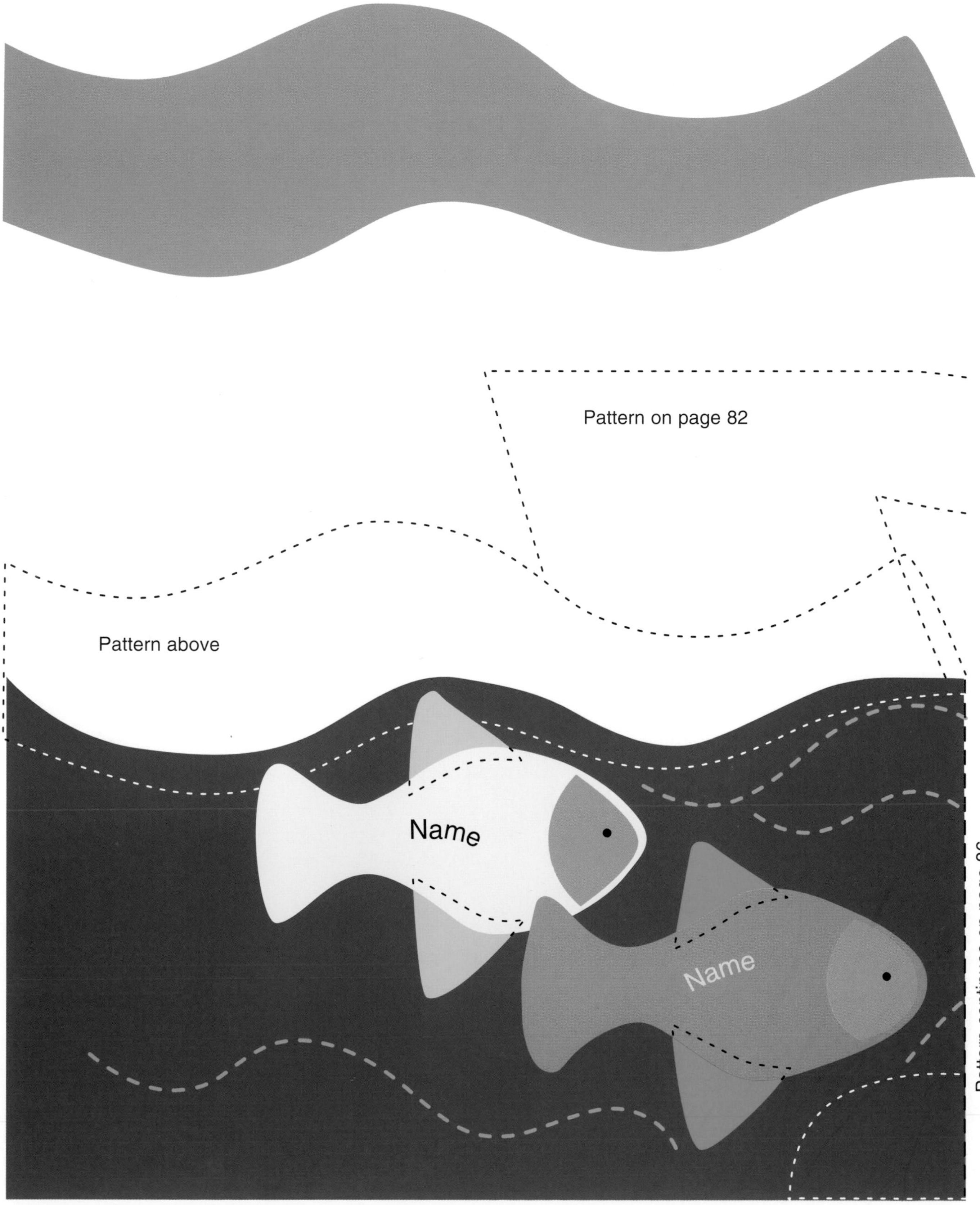
Pattern on page 82
Pattern above
Name
Name
Pattern continues on page 86

A B C D E F G H I J
K L M N O P Q R S T
U V W X Y Z
a b c d e f g h i j k l m
n o p q r s t u v w x y z
1 2 3 4 5 6 7 8 9 0

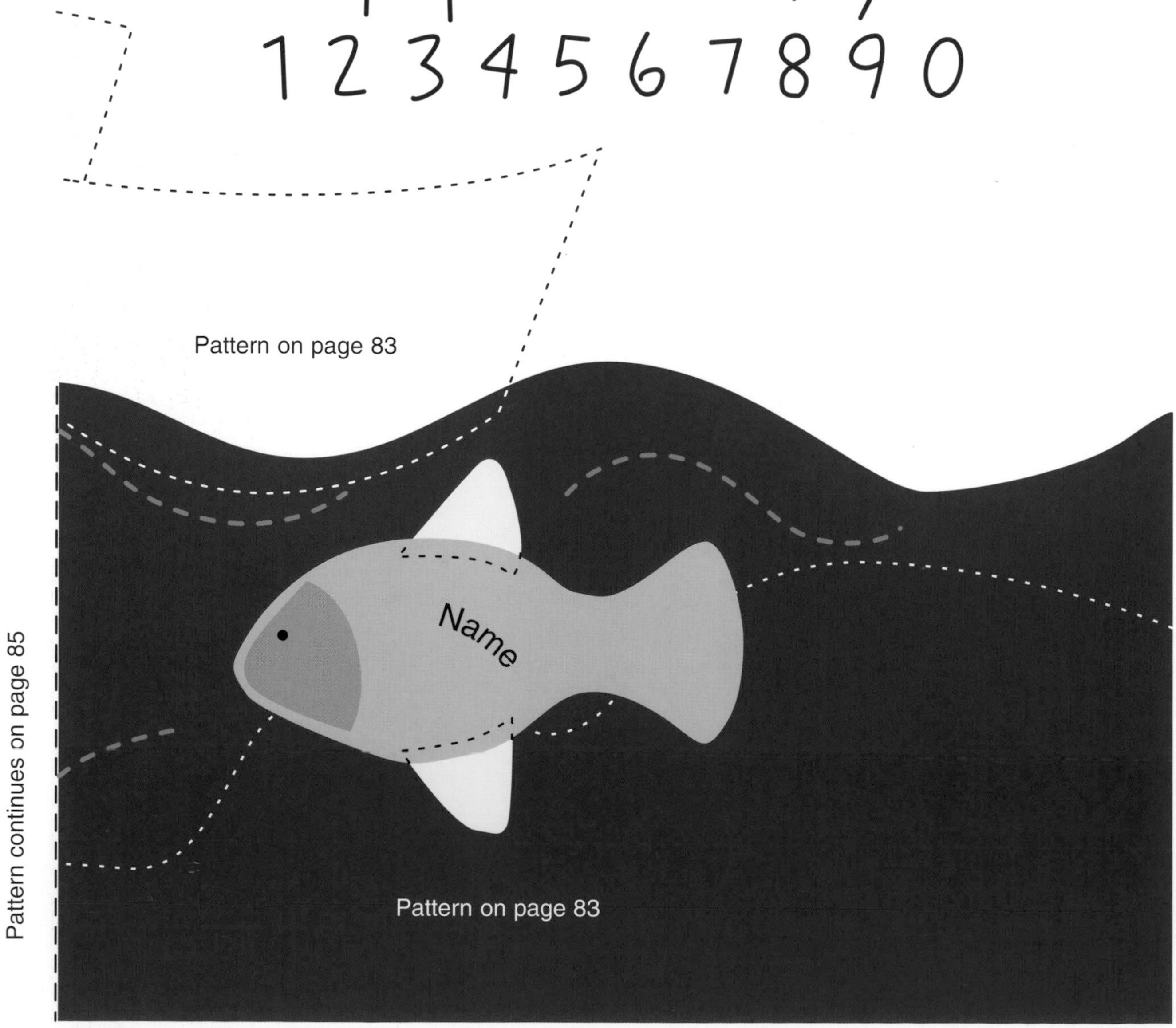

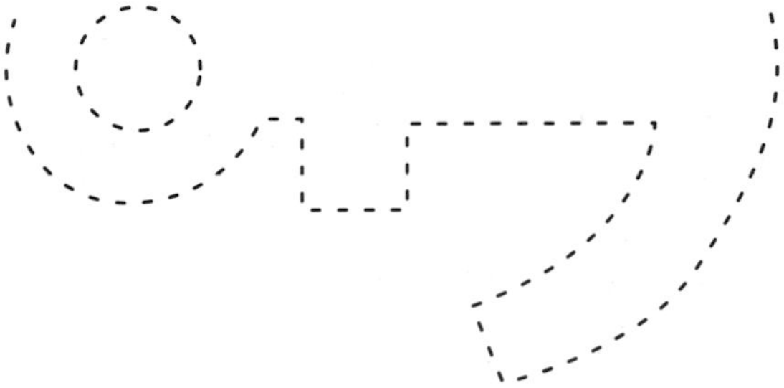

Married

Date

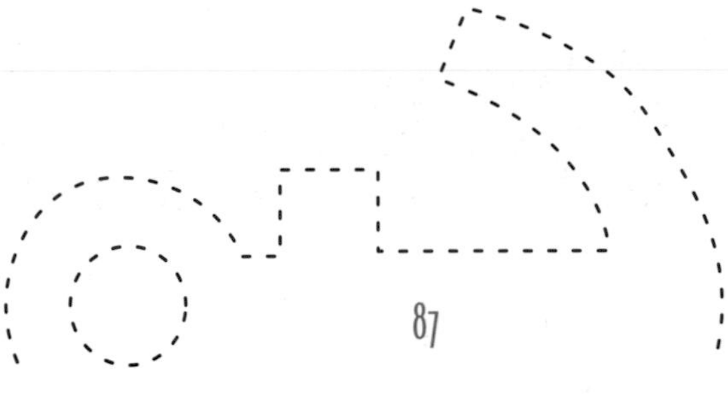

Cat on Roof

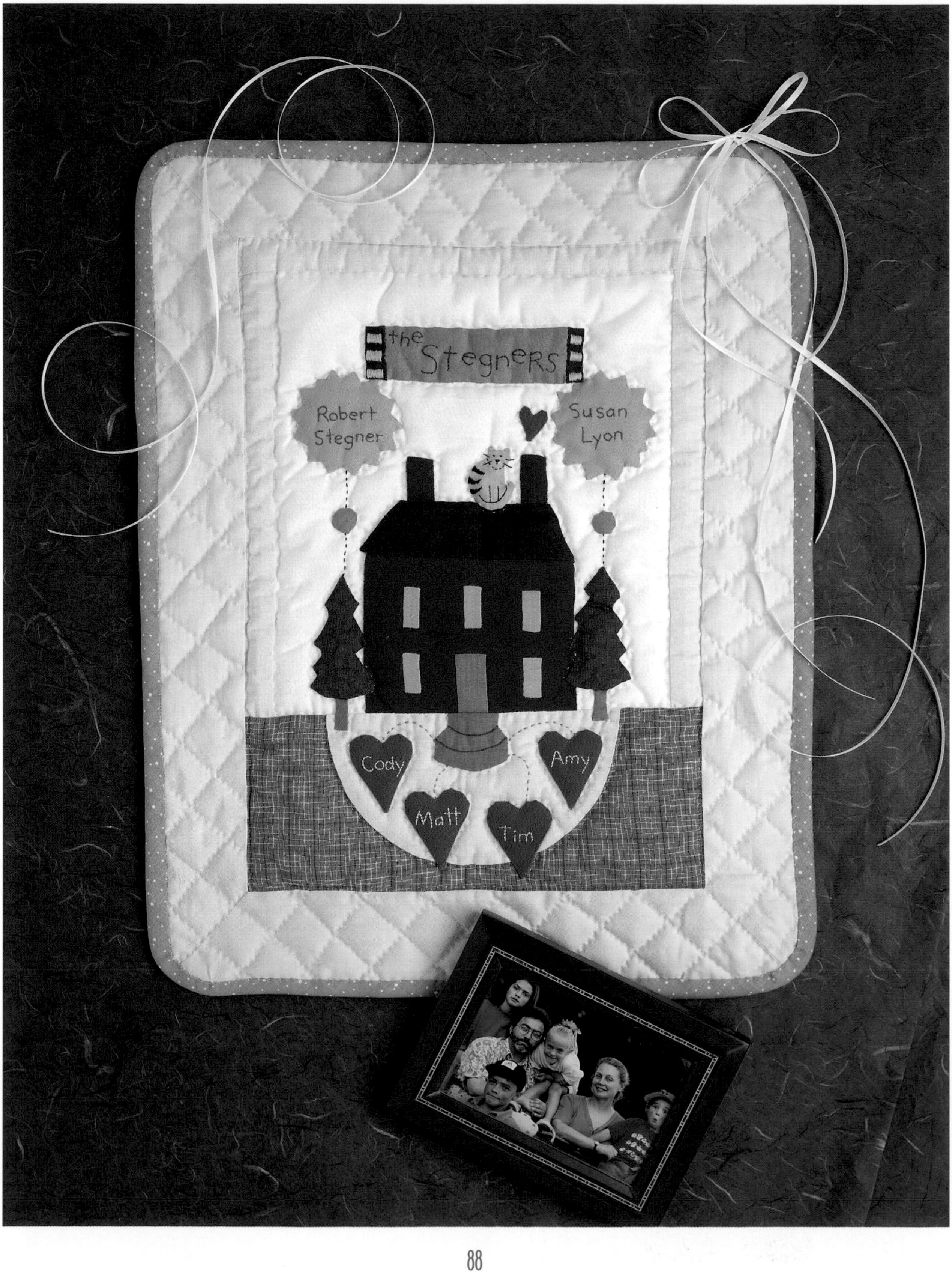

Finished size: 14" x 18"

Materials

⅝ yard pink fabric for border and backing
1 fat quarter soft green print fabric for binding
11" x 11" piece of pale green fabric for borders and semicircle
Scraps of cotton fabric in these colors: dark green, olive, 4½" x 10" scrap of green plaid, pale pink, navy blue, gray, light blue, rose, 9" x 10" scrap of pale pink, purple, brown, and gold
16" x 20" piece of polyester fleece
Thread to match fabrics (except pink, pale pink, and green print)
Embroidery floss in pale blue, navy blue, gold, black, and blue
Pink quilting thread
⅜" dowel, 16" long

Appliqué the Design

Note: Refer to "Needle-Turn Appliqué" on pages 5–6. Refer to the project photo and pattern for placement.

1. Trace the patterns individually onto tracing paper. Cut out along the lines. Pin each pattern piece to right side of the desired fabric, mark, and cut out, adding ¼" all around.
2. If your pale pink fabric is larger than 9" x 10", trim it to these exact measurements now. Center the purple house on the lower edge of the pink piece, and pin or baste. Appliqué the sides only.
3. Appliqué the 2 chimneys, then the roof, door, and windows.

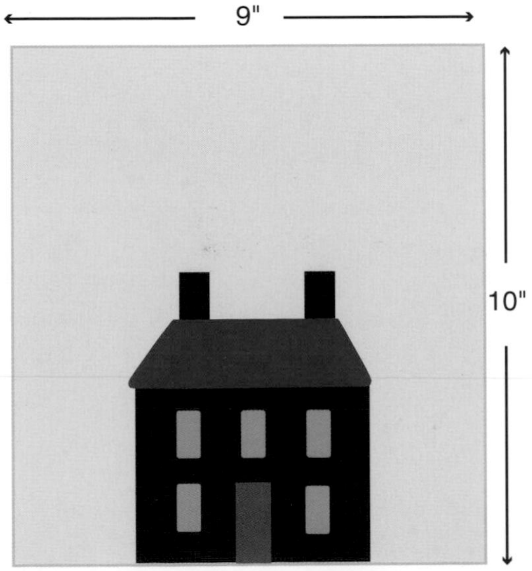

4. Appliqué the 2 light blue medallions, the olive banner (long edges only), and the 2 navy blue banner ends. Appliqué the 2 small green circles, the small heart, and the cat. Set aside.

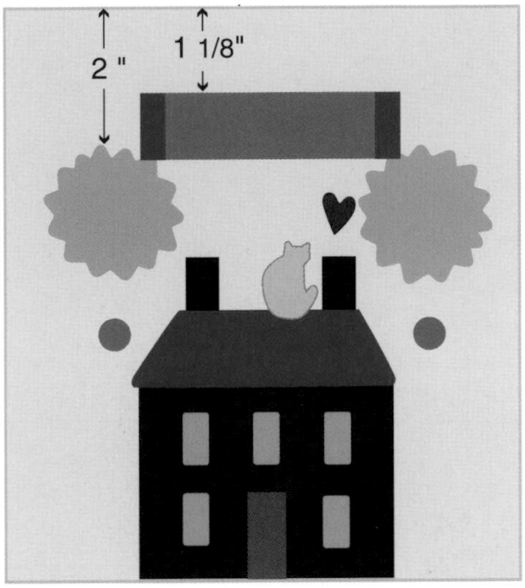

5. If your green plaid fabric is larger than 4½" x 10", trim it to these exact measurements now. Center the pale green semicircle on one 10" edge. Appliqué the curved edge only.
6. Center the gray steps on the same edge. Appliqué the side and lower edges only. Appliqué the 4 hearts. *Note: For a different number of children, simply add or subtract hearts, then place in a pleasing arrangement, pin, and appliqué.*

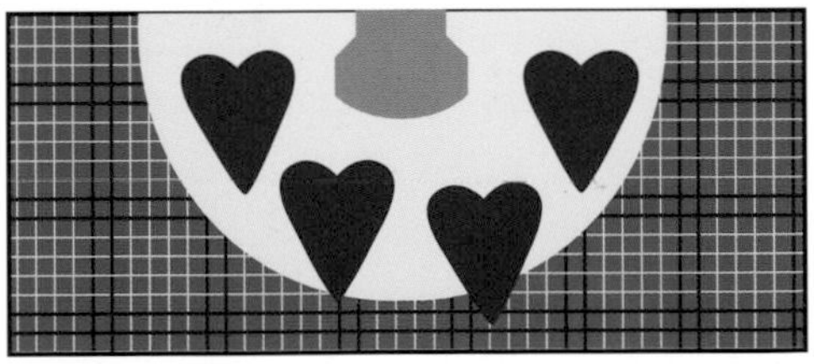

Finish the Design

1. From the pale green fabric, cut 3 strips, each 1" x 10". Sew 1 strip to each side of the pale pink background. Sew the remaining strip to the top edge.

2. Sew the green print appliquéd piece to the lower edge.
3. Appliqué a tree trunk and a tree to each side of the house.

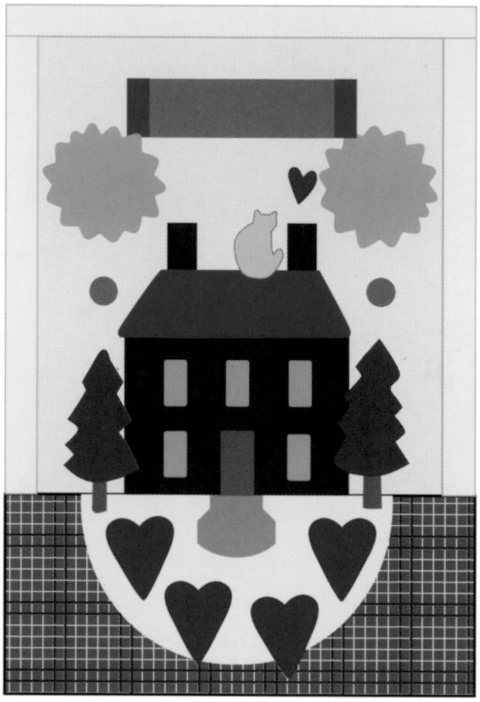

Add the Details

Note: Refer to "Adding the Details" on pages 8–11. Refer to the project photo and pattern for placement.

1. Using an air-soluble or water-soluble pen, draw all of the embroidery lines freehand. Using your chosen method, transfer the word "the" and the names in each of the spaces indicated.
2. Using 1 strand of pale blue floss, backstitch a name in each heart.
3. Using 1 strand of navy blue floss, backstitch the names in the banner and circles, and stem-stitch the curved lines in the steps.
4. Using 2 strands of gold floss, satin-stitch the bars on the edges of the banner.
5. Using 1 strand of black floss, sew a vertical line of running stitches above each tree.
6. Using 1 strand of black floss, sew running stitches along the cat's chin, backstitch the lines for the legs and tail, and satin-stitch the stripes and nose. Make a French knot for each eye. Make a long straight stitch for each whisker.
7. Using 1 strand of blue floss, connect each heart to the steps with a running stitch.

Finish the Wall Hanging

Note: Refer to "Mitering Corners" on page 7.

1. From the pink fabric, cut the following:
   2 strips, each 2¼" x 15"
   2 strips, each 2¼" x 20"
   1 piece, 16" x 20", for the backing
2. Pin to mark the midpoint of each pink strip and the midpoint of each edge of the sampler.
3. Pin a 15" pink strip to the top edge of the sampler, right sides together and midpoints matching. Stitch the pieces together, starting and stopping ¼" from the corners of the sampler. Repeat to sew the remaining 15" pink strip to the bottom edge.
4. Repeat step 3 to sew the 20" pink strips to each side of the sampler. Be sure to start and stop your stitching at the previous seams. Press.
5. Miter the corners. Trim and press.
6. Using an air-soluble or water-soluble pen, mark diagonal quilting lines 1" apart on the pink border.
7. Lay the pink backing flat, wrong side up, and lay the fleece on top. Center the sampler, right side up, on the fleece. Baste.
8. Using pink thread, quilt all the lines marked in step 6. Trim the fleece and backing to match the sampler top.
9. From the green fabric, cut 2¾"-wide bias strips, piecing as needed to yield 2 yards. Fold the bias strip in half lengthwise and press. Pin the strip to the right side of the quilted piece, raw edges matching. Machine-stitch all around, gently rounding each corner. To complete the binding, fold the strip to the wrong side and slip-stitch in place.
10. Display on a tabletop or tack to your wall. Or, to add a hanging sleeve, see the directions on page 44, but use a 2" x 13½" strip of fabric.

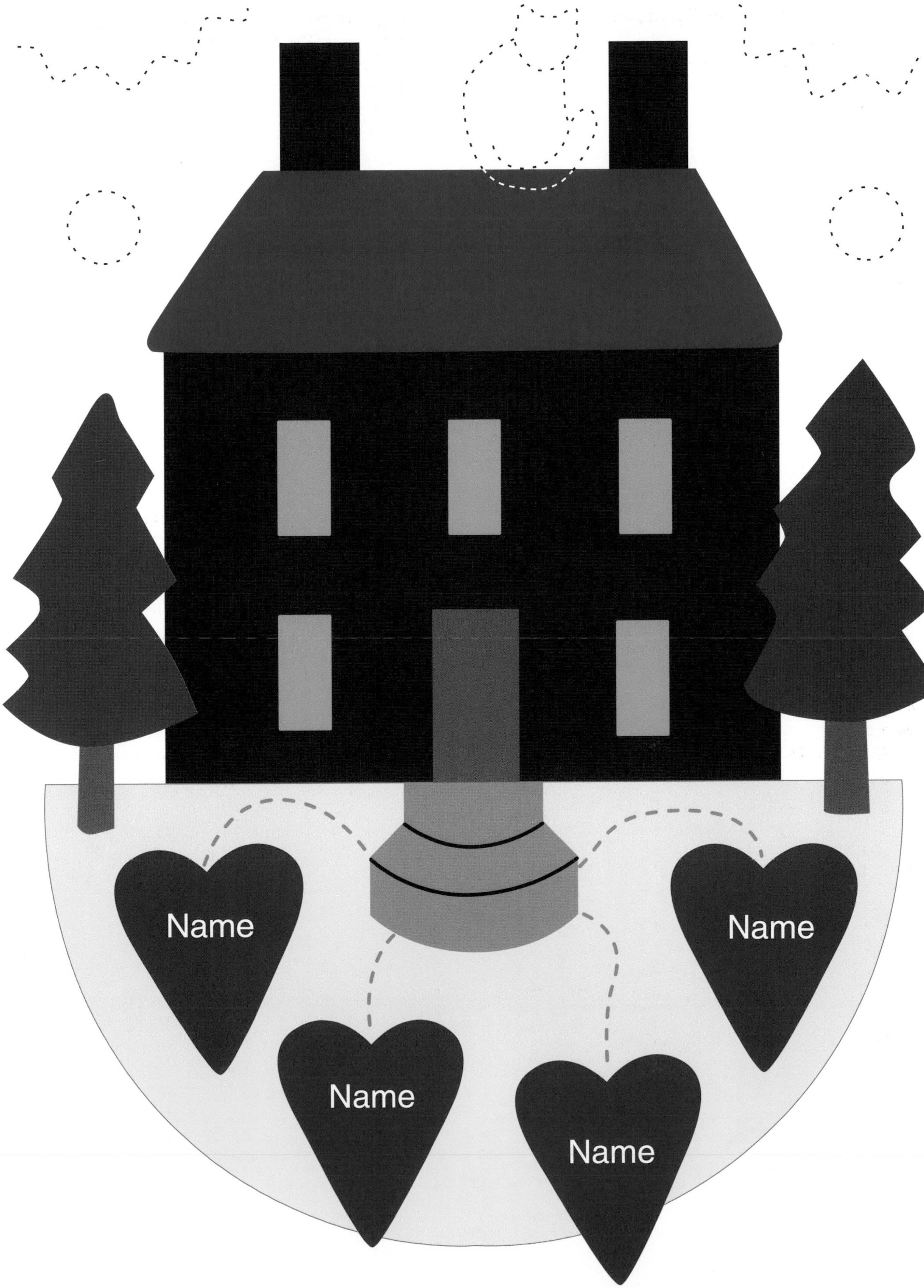
Name
Name
Name
Name

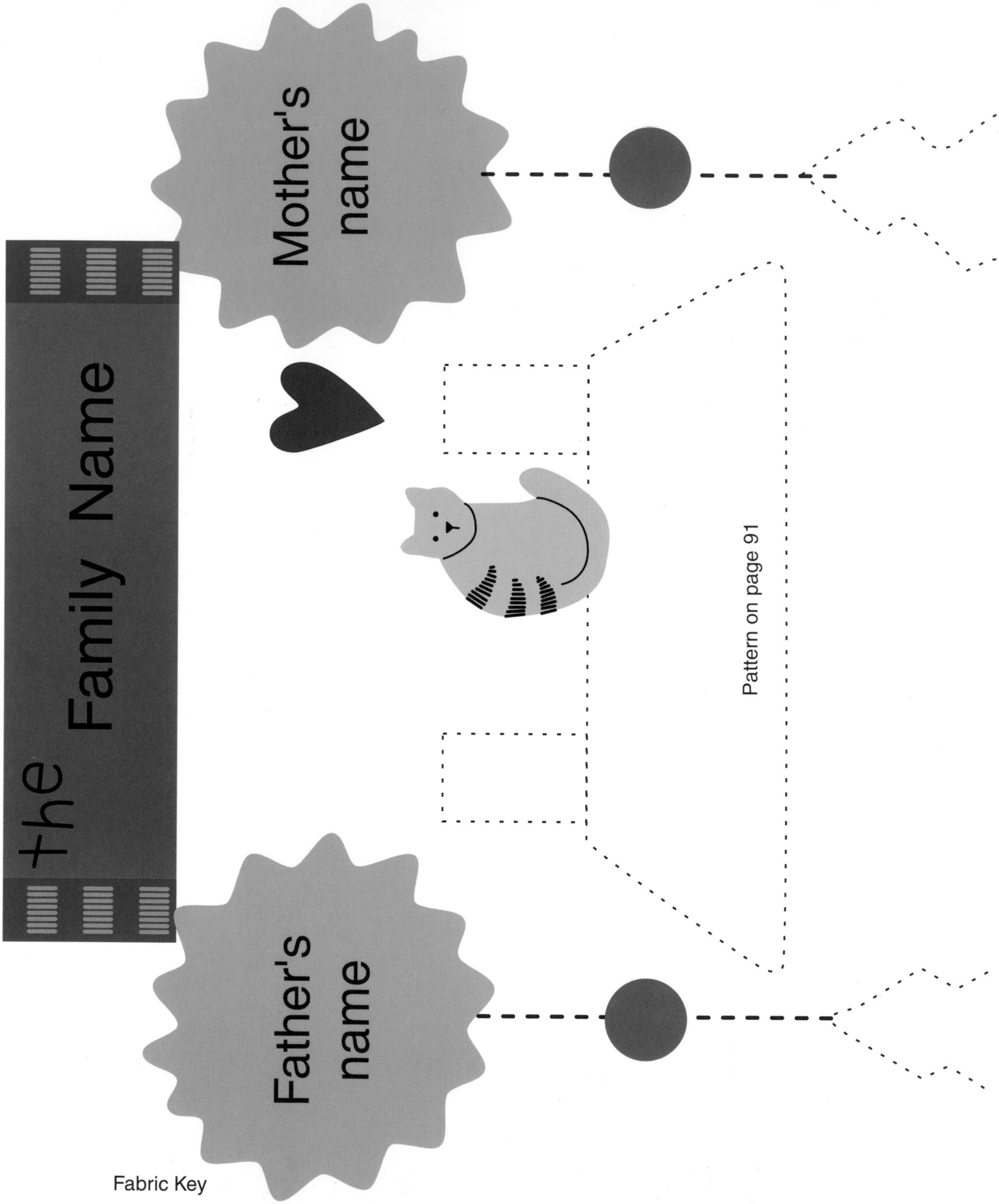

Fabric Key

Dark green	Navy blue	Pale pink
Olive green	Gray	Purple
Green plaid	Light blue	Brown
Pale green	Rose	Gold

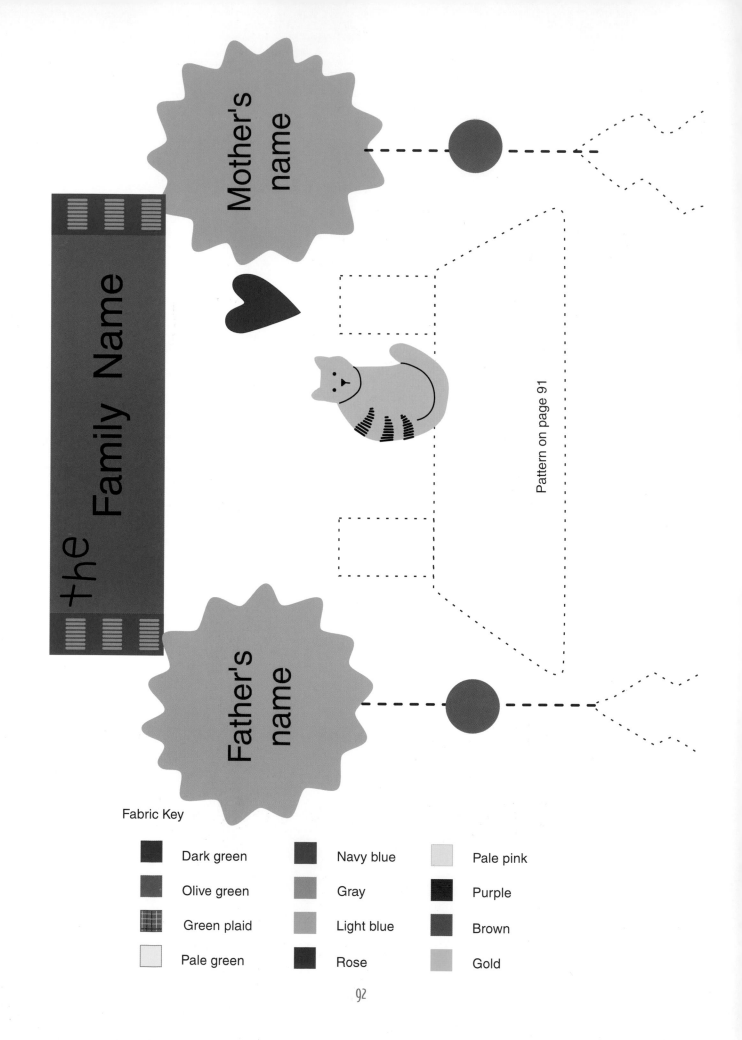

ABCDEFGHIJKL
MNOPQRSTUV
WXYZ
ABCDEFGHIJK
LMNOPQRSTU
VWXYZ
abcdefghijklmn
opqrstuvwxyz

About the Authors

With more than thirty-five years of design experience to their credit, Terrece Beesley and Trice Boerens have designed for *Better Homes and Gardens*, Oxmoor House, Leisure Arts, the American School of Needlework, *Woman's Day*, and Coats and Clark.

Trice is well known for her contemporary twists on traditional quiltmaking designs. She works in numerous artistic media, including quilting, watercolor, wood, and printmaking. Terrece co-founded the Vanessa-Ann Collection, a leading company in the needlework and craft industry for many years. More than one hundred publications showcase her design talents.

Terrece and Trice have published four other books with Martingale & Company: *Garden Appliqué*, *Fabric Mosaics*, *Appliqué for Baby*, and *Fun with Sunbonnet Sue*.

Martingale & Company
Toll-free: 1-800-426-3126

International: 1-425-483-3313
24-Hour Fax: 1-425-486-7596

PO Box 118, Bothell, WA 98041-0118 USA

Web site: www.patchwork.com
E-mail: info@martingale-pub.com

Books from Martingale & Company

These books are available through your local quilt, fabric, craft-supply, or art-supply store. For more information, contact us for a free full-color catalog. You can also find our full catalog of books online at www.patchwork.com.

That Patchwork Place® | Fiber Studio Press® | Pastimes™

Appliqué
Appliqué for Baby
Appliqué in Bloom
Baltimore Bouquets
Basic Quiltmaking Techniques for Hand Appliqué
Basic Quiltmaking Techniques for Machine Appliqué
Coxcomb Quilt
The Easy Art of Appliqué
Folk Art Animals
Fun with Sunbonnet Sue
Garden Appliqué
The Nursery Rhyme Quilt
Red and Green: An Appliqué Tradition
Rose Sampler Supreme
Stars in the Garden
Sunbonnet Sue All Through the Year

Beginning Quiltmaking
Basic Quiltmaking Techniques for Borders & Bindings
Basic Quiltmaking Techniques for Curved Piecing
Basic Quiltmaking Techniques for Divided Circles
Basic Quiltmaking Techniques for Eight-Pointed Stars
Basic Quiltmaking Techniques for Hand Appliqué
Basic Quiltmaking Techniques for Machine Appliqué
Basic Quiltmaking Techniques for Strip Piecing
The Quilter's Handbook
Your First Quilt Book (or it should be!)

Crafts
15 Beads
Fabric Mosaics
Folded Fabric Fun
Making Memories

Cross-Stitch & Embroidery
Hand-Stitched Samplers from I Done My Best
Kitties to Stitch and Quilt: 15 Redwork Designs
Miniature Baltimore Album Quilts
A Silk-Ribbon Album

Designing Quilts
Color: The Quilter's Guide
Design Essentials: The Quilter's Guide
Design Your Own Quilts
Designing Quilts: The Value of Value
The Nature of Design
QuiltSkills
Sensational Settings
Surprising Designs from Traditional Quilt Blocks
Whimsies & Whynots

Holiday
Christmas Ribbonry
Easy Seasonal Wall Quilts
Favorite Christmas Quilts from That Patchwork Place
Holiday Happenings
Quilted for Christmas
Quilted for Christmas, Book IV
Special-Occasion Table Runners
Welcome to the North Pole

Home Decorating
The Home Decorator's Stamping Book
Make Room for Quilts
Special-Occasion Table Runners
Stitch & Stencil
Welcome Home: Debbie Mumm
Welcome Home: Kaffe Fassett

Knitting
Simply Beautiful Sweaters
Two Sticks and a String

Paper Arts
The Art of Handmade Paper and Collage
Grow Your Own Paper
Stamp with Style

Paper Piecing
Classic Quilts with Precise Foundation Piecing
Easy Machine Paper Piecing
Easy Mix & Match Machine Paper Piecing
Easy Paper-Pieced Keepsake Quilts
Easy Paper-Pieced Miniatures
Easy Reversible Vests
Go Wild with Quilts
Go Wild with Quilts—Again!
It's Raining Cats & Dogs
Mariner's Medallion
Needles and Notions
Paper-Pieced Curves
Paper Piecing the Seasons
A Quilter's Ark
Sewing on the Line
Show Me How to Paper Piece

Quilting & Finishing Techniques
The Border Workbook
Borders by Design
A Fine Finish
Happy Endings
Interlacing Borders
Lap Quilting Lives!
Loving Stitches
Machine Quilting Made Easy
Quilt It!
Quilting Design Sourcebook
Quilting Makes the Quilt
The Ultimate Book of Quilt Labels

Ribbonry
Christmas Ribbonry
A Passion for Ribbonry
Wedding Ribbonry

Rotary Cutting & Speed Piecing
101 Fabulous Rotary-Cut Quilts
365 Quilt Blocks a Year Perpetual Calendar
All-Star Sampler
Around the Block with Judy Hopkins
Basic Quiltmaking Techniques for Strip Piecing
Beyond Log Cabin
Block by Block
Easy Stash Quilts
Fat Quarter Quilts
The Joy of Quilting
A New Twist on Triangles
A Perfect Match
Quilters on the Go
ScrapMania
Shortcuts
Simply Scrappy Quilts
Spectacular Scraps
Square Dance
Stripples Strikes Again!
Strips That Sizzle
Surprising Designs from Traditional Quilt Blocks
Traditional Quilts with Painless Borders
Time-Crunch Quilts
Two-Color Quilts

Small & Miniature Quilts
Bunnies by the Bay Meets Little Quilts
Celebrate! With Little Quilts
Easy Paper-Pieced Miniatures
Fun with Miniature Log Cabin Blocks
Little Quilts all Through the House
Living with Little Quilts
Miniature Baltimore Album Quilts
A Silk-Ribbon Album
Small Quilts Made Easy
Small Wonders

Surface Design
Complex Cloth
Creative Marbling on Fabric
Dyes & Paints
Fantasy Fabrics
Hand-Dyed Fabric Made Easy
Jazz It Up
Machine Quilting with Decorative Threads
New Directions in Chenille
Thread Magic
Threadplay with Libby Lehman

Topics in Quiltmaking
Bargello Quilts
The Cat's Meow
Even More Quilts for Baby
Everyday Angels in Extraordinary Quilts
Fabric Collage Quilts
Fast-and-Fun Stenciled Quilts
Folk Art Quilts
It's Raining Cats & Dogs
Kitties to Stitch and Quilt: 15 Redwork Designs
Life in the Country with Country Threads
Machine-Stitched Cathedral Windows
More Quilts for Baby
A New Slant on Bargello Quilts
Patchwork Pantry
Pink Ribbon Quilts
Quilted Landscapes
The Quilted Nursery
Quilting Your Memories
Quilts for Baby
Quilts from Aunt Amy
Whimsies & Whynots

Watercolor Quilts
More Strip-Pieced Watercolor Magic
Quick Watercolor Quilts
Strip-Pieced Watercolor Magic
Watercolor Impressions
Watercolor Quilts

Wearables
Easy Reversible Vests
Just Like Mommy
New Directions in Chenille
Quick-Sew Fleece
Variations in Chenille

1/00